Residences Reimagined

Successful Renovation and Expansion of Old Homes

Residences Reimagined

Successful Renovation and Expansion of Old Homes

Publishing

CONTENTS

007 **On Domestic Archaeology**

010 '60s Modern Renovation

018 Cal Jordi Anna

026 Edinburgh Pavilion

032 Tower House

042 Rathgar House

052 St Kilda Cottage House

060 Picture Frame House

068 FK House

076 Hillside Midcentury

086 Light Falls

096 Mibunakagawa House

104 Shanghai Xuhui Old House Renovation and Interior Design

114 The Journey House

122 Beira Mar House

132 House Between Pillars

140 Residence for Biju Mathew

148 RaeRae House

158 Maisonette in Notting Hill

166 House C

172 House in Hanegi

178 House for Four Generations

188 Candid House

196 House in Oyamazaki

206 Villa Kuro

220 House Renovation in Montcada

226 The Furnished Void

232 Photographer's House

238 **INDEX**

Francesco Pierazzi

Francesco Pierazzi has worked for over twenty years, designing architecture internationally in Italy, Germany, and now London.

During his time in Italy, he worked on a variety of projects, ranging from high-end retail outlets to mixed-use schemes, as well as one-off houses.

Francesco relocated to London in 2002 to join Charles Barclay Architects to work on high-end domestic projects throughout London. His participation in international design competitions has been significant, leading many different projects, including the RIBA award-winning Kielder Observatory in Northumberland. He also worked at Brady Mallalieu Architects and Charles Tashima Architecture.

Francesco Pierazzi Architects was established in London in 2014, with a body of work that includes a variety of domestic projects, both in London and abroad.

ON DOMESTIC ARCHAEOLOGY

My profession has, more often than not, forced me to reimagine and reinvent buildings that already exist, whether by means of a conversion, or an extension, or through small and well-crafted interferences.

Occasionally, I have designed a simpler remodeling or have worked with spaces that needed only to be lightly upgraded.

Despite the complexity or modesty of these interventions, I have utilized each project as an opportunity to look back at the past and reflect upon it, be it my own professional past—former projects that still resonate many years after their completion—or the past of anything that has offered me inspiration: a novel, an artwork, a movie, or a building.

I embrace the saying that "without the past, there is no future." Despite my delving and research, the origins of this phrase remain a mystery still. Through time, authors have paraphrased it or attempted to reimagine its significance and make the saying their own; the gist and fact of it is: to understand where we are heading, we must know where we have come from.

Carl Elefante became famous, among other things, for coining the phrase that the greenest building is the one that is already built. Recently, I felt that I needed to refer once again to those pages that appeared in the *Forum Journal* in the summer of 2007, to remind me that any argument that concerns the merits of repurposing the expansive building stock must, undeniably, stem from the pressure to fight climate change. And that, while it has now become apparent that to effectively attempt to deal with the climate emergency we must build more sustainably, we also have to take care of the existing assets and embrace them for the way they contribute to their contexts, and to our lives at large.

This is not true only because we know that building replacement necessitates high-energy consumption, but more importantly, also because we can grasp the opportunity of a different design approach, which may in turn contribute to the appreciation of different aesthetics.

Sustainability is evolving rapidly and designers must reimagine buildings with an upcycling approach, and embrace the responsibility to produce artifacts of higher qualities and values than those of the original buildings. In shaping the built environment, we shape our lives.

I like to compare this process to the Rose of Jericho, or similar resurrection plants. This small moss-like plant has a grayish foliage and the ability to survive a long period of dehydration, entering a dormancy-like state that takes place in the summer months. To the untrained eye, the plant may appear deprived of life when curled up, only to spring back to life when the right environmental conditions are met.

I often use this type of parallel as a source of inspiration when I begin to strategize a new project.

The pages of Jun'ichirō Tanizaki's *Sasameyuki* (*The Makioka Sisters* in English) and the lingering feeling of impermanence that permeates the novel have regularly impacted my work. Similarly, the sculptural geometric abstractions of artist Jan Schoonhoven have inspired a suburban timber extension and the philosophy of Maurice Merleau-Ponty—when he argues about the role that perception plays in understanding the world, and that the body is the primary site of knowing it—has contributed heavily in the transformation of a maisonette in London's Notting Hill.

My work is predominantly based in London, where Victorian unlisted terraced houses—within or outside Conservation Areas—constitute a considerable part of the housing stock. They are now a defining feature of the urban fabric throughout the many boroughs of the city, and of some suburban enclaves.

For those not in the know, their designs are consistently very similar, with nearly identical floor plans and repetitive architectural details that were often sourced from pattern books, both for their exteriors and their interiors.

When I moved from a rare London modernist 1937 purpose-built flat to a late-1800s ubiquitous Victorian terrace in a southeast district of the city, I discovered that the original owners had "reimagined" their home in 1973, when DIY practices were rampant throughout the United Kingdom, which gave every family the possibility of keeping up appearances despite dwindling income.

The familiar predicament of how to repurpose a building type that may, or may not, have already exhausted its limited mutations, became (in the instance of the terrace), the opportunity to release and celebrate the history

of the former inhabitants by incorporating and reinterpreting the aesthetics that had guided the owners' 1970s renovation.

I began the design process by surgically removing and cataloguing some forty different samples of materials and finishes that ranged from faux ceramic tiles to patterned shag-pile carpets, and cork tiles to brick-patterned wallpapers, not discounting polystyrene geometric ceiling tiles and net curtains of varied designs.

With the components taken apart, the project began to tell a story by taking a different approach; and by letting the existing structure play a leading role in the design, the house was almost—to a degree— designing itself.

With no scope for a bold architectural gesture, the significance of this approach is directed at empowering the users, rather than the public.

This practice of domestic archaeology, founded on shared human experiences, is a creative process that wishes to produce an output that is guided by a profound respect for the environment, recognizing that sustainability is a necessity, and acknowledging that well-crafted projects are timeless.

At times, when it is apparent that some designs may place too strong an emphasis on their short-lived novelty, to be able to reimagine enduring buildings that can withstand the test of time—that are guided by solid and established design principles, and which distance themselves from finite trends that will be, by definition, short-lived—is the most sustainable way to ensure that architects and designers not only focus on the design of longer-lasting building components, but also make certain that their final products last as long as possible.

By tying in with the past, the present can mature into a continuum where old and new can either blend seamlessly into one another or make a statement.

And while I am a proponent of the re-use of many existing buildings on the grounds of sustainability, and advocate that they should be upgraded to be as efficient as they can possibly be—regardless of the building type and the climate in which they reside—I strongly support the idea that they deserve to be reinvented, on the basis that their stories may not just yet have been entirely told.

'60s MODERN RENOVATION

Location:
Gold Coast, Australia
Area:
3,323 square feet (309 square meters)
Completion:
2015
Design:
Jamison Architects
Photography:
Remco Photography

This renovation project was met with challenges from the outset, courtesy of a list of site and building constraints that were paired with an ambitious design response to make the most of the site's unique locality and beauty.

Set in the upper apartment of an original early '80s duplex building located on the side of a steep hill (the site drops away from beneath it), the house presented difficult site access. There were also issues of fire separation logistics and town planning requirements to contend with. The clients also had an extensive brief, requiring living spaces to open to the incredible view (originally restricted by a low roof and small windows) and the addition of a second story, along with a main suite and an outside entertainment area that allows the stunning location to be enjoyed. They were very involved in the design and construction, from concept to interior, and exterior selections, as well as finishing touches, making the renovation very personal.

The new double-height living area features an expansive northern window that opens up to views of the Pacific Ocean and the Gold Coast skyline. Articulated with thoughtful glazing solutions, the façade is also veiled in decorative screening, aiding in both sun control and privacy; it can be adapted to suit the clients' requirements as needed. Operable louvers connect the interior to the exterior green environment while still maintaining privacy from neighbors.

The new main suite is expansive and luxurious, and includes a bedroom, lounge retreat, joinery, en suite, and walk-in wardrobe. It can be opened to connect with the covered entertainment terrace and lounge retreat, or screened off for privacy, creating a very versatile and usable space.

This project was about the clients having a dream, and the architectural design has created the feeling and spaces to make that dream come true, enabling them to enjoy the lifestyle they wished for.

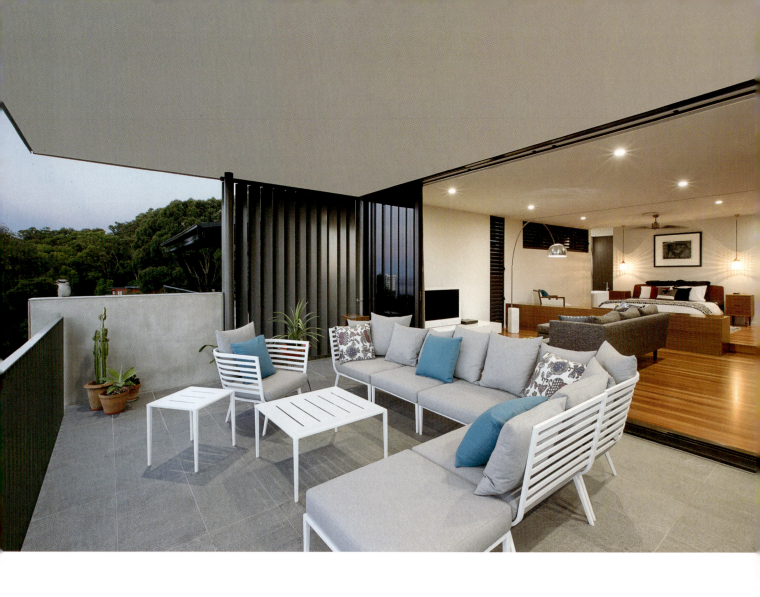

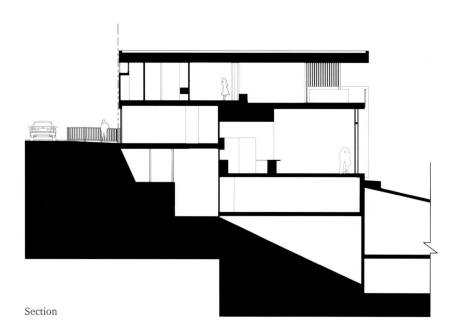

Section

Second-floor plan

First-floor plan

CAL JORDI ANNA

Location:
El Poal, Catalonia, Spain
Area:
3,261 square feet (303 square meters)
Completion:
2018
Design:
Hiha Studio
Photography:
Pol Viladoms

This project is an update of an existing building to adapt it to new materials, the present, and importantly, to new ways of life.

The existing building is the sum of two houses between rammed-earth party walls. These buildings respond to the typology in the La Plana de Lleida area and feature a plot that is around 16 feet (5 meters) wide and 49 to 98 feet (15 to 30 meters) long.

The main approach empties the existing building in a selective way, in order to attain project aims and provide for functional needs. This "emptying" eliminated elements and reduced remodeling, thereby enabling expenses to stretch economically.

The reduced remodeling generates new visuals and relationships between the new rooms, both vertically and horizontally. Placing the empty spaces in contact with the north and south façades allows a greater contact surface with the exterior, creating a more compact building. This reduced depth extends the light channeled in from the façade to the center of the house.

The design is targeted toward giving the new spaces a domestic feel in the face of their monumentality. Public spaces are set in the new inner spaces generated by the selective clearing of the interior. They are visual connectors, even though they are set at different levels. In them, day-to-day life takes place; the more private areas are located around these rooms.

There are three levels in this home. On the first floor, visitors can be greeted by the "Roman Fauces" entrance, in tribute to the large entrance halls of the farmhouses and traditional houses in the town. Day activities are concentrated on the second floor, with the living room, kitchen, and dining room linked to the inner terrace and bathroom and accompanying room. The third floor is used as the evening/night space; it is where bedrooms and their adjoining bathrooms are concentrated.

The material essence of housing is achieved by stripping and removing all ornaments and finishes prior to remodeling, and returning the building to its original appearance. The aim was to recover the essence of the house typology, where material, texture, and color are given additional value and incorporated within the new interior language. The rammed-earth walls take on a prominent technical role in this new language as they regulate the natural moisture, temperature, and acoustics of the home's interior.

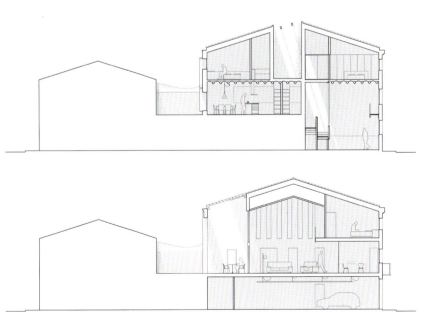

Sections

Second-floor plan

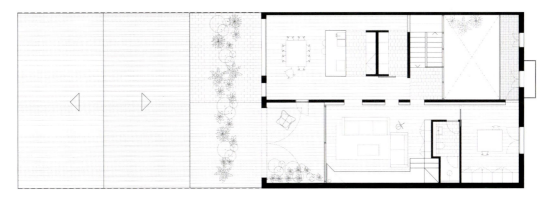

First-floor plan

EDINBURGH PAVILION

Location:
Edinburgh, Scotland
Area:
5,059 square feet (470 square meters)
Completion:
2019
Design:
Archer + Braun
Photography:
David Barbour

In this project, an expanding family required the renovation of the existing home to include a new open-plan kitchen that welcomes light, and a dining space suited to modern living, with a connection to the garden.

The existing property consisted of a series of grand rooms with decorative features that were arranged in a formal manner, typical of Victorian villas. A glazed rectangular volume with minimal structural intervention allows an open plan that floods the interior with light, while being a deliberate contrast to the historic property. Leading from the entrance hall, an axial view allows glimpses into the extension through to the garden beyond—accessed via sliding, glazed wall panels, which open up the layout. A glazed link (consisting of frameless fixed glass) separates the existing building from the new extension.

Most of the original rooms are retained, with reconfiguration focusing on the secondary spaces to the rear of the house, so as to create the "back of house" rooms to serve the new extension.

Specification and detailing of materials that supported the minimal aesthetic was key to the design. Superfluous detailing is reduced and the steel structural system is discrete, with the columns set back from the façades and corners; the glazing runs past the roof build-up to create a slim coping detail.

The stone walls of the pavilion are structured from locally sourced warm-red and fine-grained sandstone that has been used in some of Edinburgh's most recognizable buildings, such as the Scottish National Portrait Gallery. The detailing and specification of the stonework ensure a contemporary and monolithic aesthetic, while reinterpreting the traditional stonemason techniques seen on the existing property. Large-format stones and matching flush mortar were selected from a specific stone band within the quarry.

The primary and secondary elevations differ in their finishes. The (primary) garden elevation displays a smooth stone façade achieved through the "rub" technique and the secondary elevations of the pavilion are grit blasted.

This technique is used as a contemporary way of referencing the rough finish of traditional stonemason techniques such as "stugging."

A key component of the new extension was using material that is long-lasting and robust, but also low in carbon. Natural stone, particularly when sourced locally—as Corsehill stone was—is a low-carbon building material compared with brick or concrete. Solid stone instead of cladding reduces the amount of concrete blockwork that is needed. The existing fabric of the building is also upgraded and features new windows, roof insulation, under-floor heating, new electrical systems, and low-energy lights throughout. Solar-control blinds are also added throughout the extension to reduce the risk of overheating because of the generous glazing incorporated.

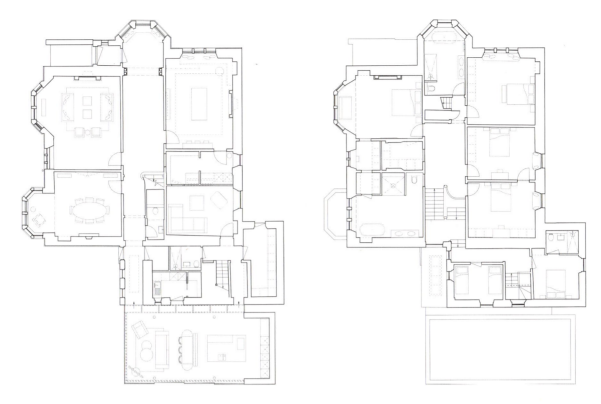

First-floor plan

Second-floor plan

TOWER HOUSE

Location:
Alphington, Victoria, Australia
Area:
2,422 square feet (225 square meters)
Completion:
2015
Design:
Austin Maynard Architects
Photography:
Peter Bennetts Studio, Tess Kelly

A renovation and extension to a weatherboard home in the suburb of Alphington restores the original house and adds a studio, bedroom, bathroom, kitchen, and dining room in the new part of the house.

The home is the result of dedicated discussions with trusting, enthusiastic, patient, and encouraging clients who have a keen interest in the environment and who enjoy outdoor recreation and the arts.

Bound by two roads—one, a leafy postwar suburban street and the other, facing backyards (and feeling like a country road)—Tower House is located near a parkland and the Yarra River, with views to the Amcor chimney stacks. Save for a few new homes, the context is mainly small weatherboard and brick homes. Based on this, the design creates a series of small structures of a certain scale and texture to create an amiable character for the home, so that it does not appear as a hostile monolith dominating the context.

This creates a house that is a village externally and a home internally. The house defies logic as the exterior appears to be a series of small structures, while internally the spaces and functions are large and connected. Because of this, what was once hidden is now fully displayed—particularly the mess on the rooftop. To overcome this flaw, Tower House is deliberately designed to look beautiful from a high viewpoint, such as Google Earth.

With streets on both sides of Tower House, neighbors can use the garden as a shortcut and grab a few vegetables on the way through; open gates blur the line between public and private.

Keeping sustainable design at its core, the house's new form runs along the southern boundary to capture natural light, instead of extruding its existing structure. Windows and openings are designed to optimize passive solar gain, thereby drastically reducing demands on mechanical heating and cooling. All windows are double glazed; white roofs drastically reduce urban heat sink and heat transfer internally. The need for air conditioning is minimized greatly through the active management of shade, as well as ample ventilation.

034

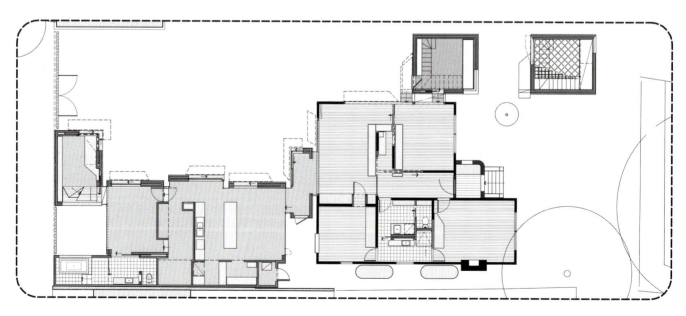

Floor plan

RATHGAR HOUSE

Location:
Dublin, Ireland
Area:
5,307 square feet (493 square meters)
Completion:
2019
Design:
Peter Legge Associates
Photography:
Aisling McCoy

This renovation and extension of a large Victorian end-of-terrace house in Rathgar, an established inner suburb in Dublin, began with stripping the upper levels to bring them back to their original features and proportions; non-flattering additions were removed, so as to reveal the essential character of the spaces.

The lower-level layout is slightly adjusted and non-original elements, a side extension, bay window, and metal balcony were removed, turning over function and circulation.

A new side-door entrance leads to an extension at the rear, which arranges an open-plan living space with direct connection to the rear garden. Though the rear extension faces north, fenestrations cleverly placed in each cardinal direction work with the large opening in the roof to draw a flood of natural light into the space that changes sequences throughout the day, creating a pleasant and inviting interior. The material palette in the interior is subdued and unobtrusive, so that the homeowner's vibrant artwork collection stands as the highlight.

The curve of the existing rear façade influences the form of the extension, which curves gently along the side access. It is finished in render with brownish brass and copper sheeting on the oak window frames and exterior reveals—the former to relate to the finish of the existing house, and the latter to complement it with a restrained luster.

The home celebrates its historic past as it stylishly flaunts an outfit adapted for contemporary life.

Section

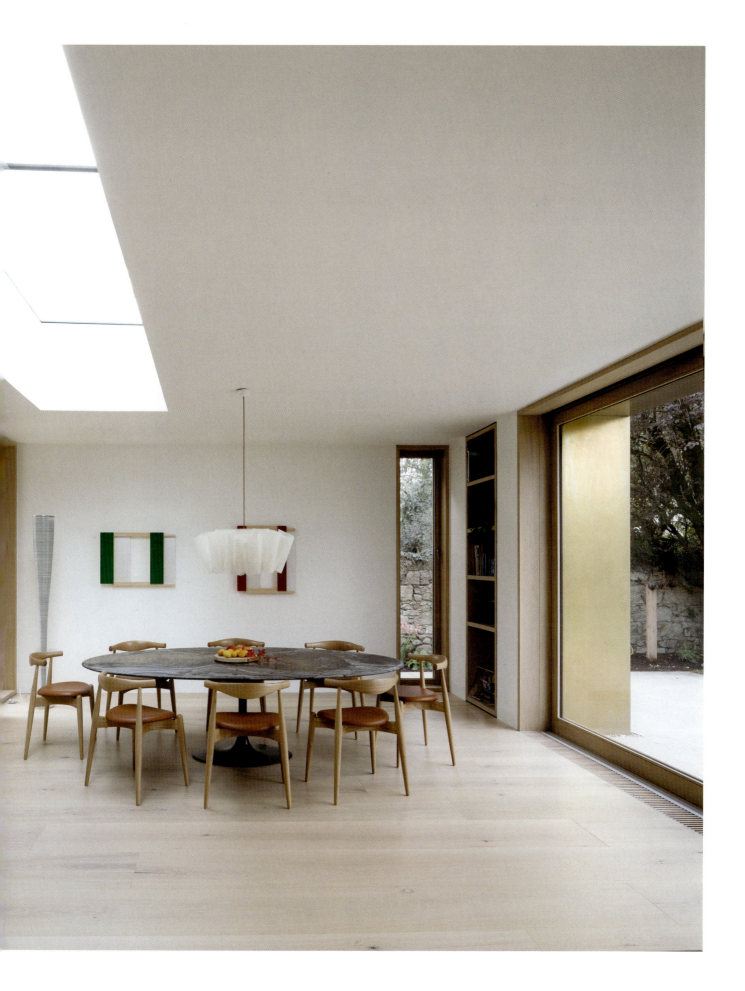

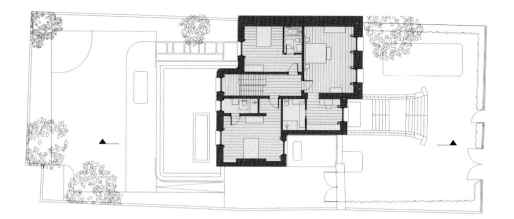

Third-floor plan

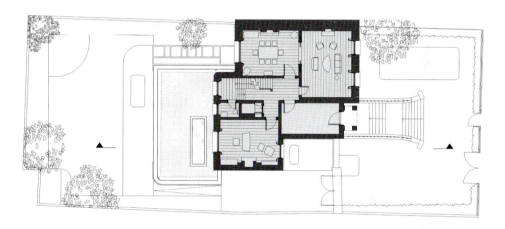

Second-floor plan

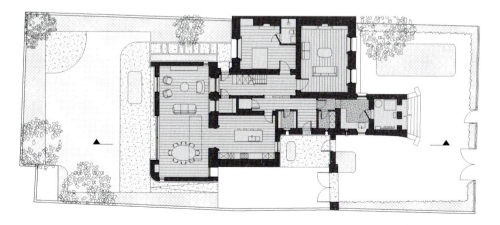

First-floor plan

ST KILDA COTTAGE HOUSE

Location:
St Kilda, Victoria, Australia

Area:
1,507 square feet (140 square meters)

Completion:
2019

Design:
Jost Architects

Photography:
Tom Roe, Shani Hodson

A classic weatherboard cottage in St Kilda gets a modern redesign that speaks of contemporary living, as it considers the environment. An earlier rear extension on the first floor is removed, while retaining the front bedrooms and a bathroom that are part of the original house. Working with the current first-floor footprint, without pushing further back to the rear, a new kitchen is added and an area of land to the northeast is utilized. The brief also adds an en-suite main bedroom, walk-in wardrobe, and an east-facing deck on the upper level, which called for a careful negotiation of the interaction with the streetscape due to planning restrictions. In order to effectively use the northeast space on the tapered site, none of the gutter line, roof ridge, and internal ceiling and wall junctions are horizontal or parallel to each other. This unconventional geometry ensures that the upper-level façades present symmetrically to either end of the property. The resulting screened internal space enveloped within the form arranges areas of visual permeability, creating an active façade that changes with the time of day and lighting.

New additions are intentionally contemporary to contrast with the original dwelling, but still respect the design heritage of the home, such as the galvanized custom orb cladding that wraps up one side and extends over and down the other, intersecting with the weatherboard cladding. Both are familiar materials usually seen on the classic Victorian workers' cottages found in this part of St Kilda.

Clever internal planning mitigates the new, reduced floor area, and incorporates a small rear yard and stair access to the upper level in an improved functional layout. A banquette seat to the front of the kitchen bench frees up valuable living space. The laundry is located in the hallway at the top of the stairs that also situates the front-facing roof deck access. Returning back along the stair void, the main bedroom is introduced, presenting a rear deck beyond. The circulation returns to the east, leading to the walk-in wardrobe and en suite, and back out to the eastern deck.

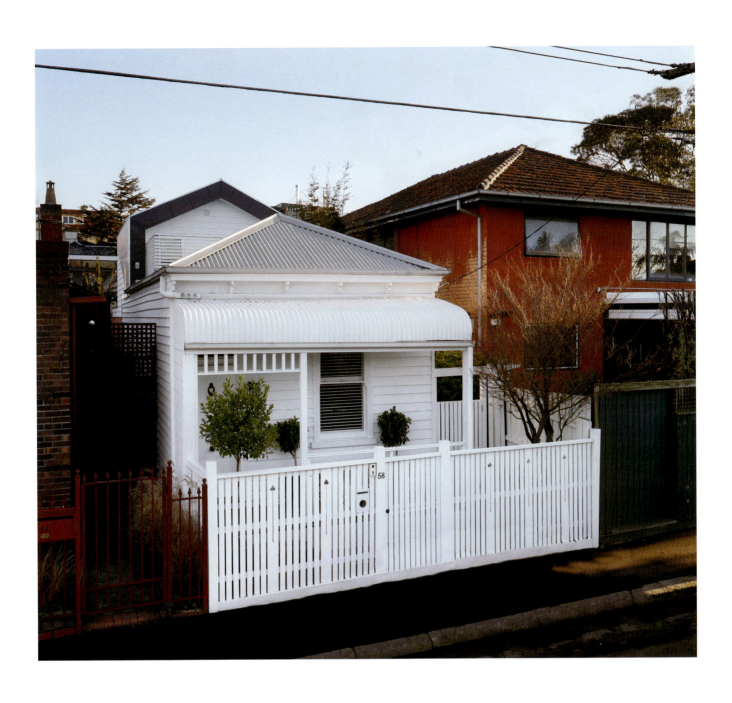

This room-to-room movement in the doughnut-shaped plan reduces the extent of wasted egress area, while designing good cross-ventilation in the rooms on the upper floor.

Interior finishes are honest to the raw textures and colors of materials used, displaying a complementary pairing of sensibility and classic functionality that won't become dated. Long-lasting and durable materials, such as decorative concrete with zoned hydronic heating, thermally broken aluminum, and narrow-profile steel frame double-glazed windows and sliding doors speak for sustainability. This is teamed with the sensible application of thermally passive design, energy-efficient lighting and fixtures, and a photovoltaic system to tailor a comfortable home with a low environmental cost.

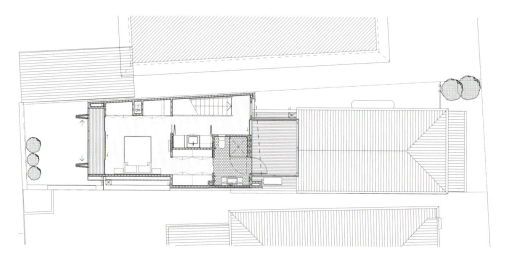

Second-floor plan

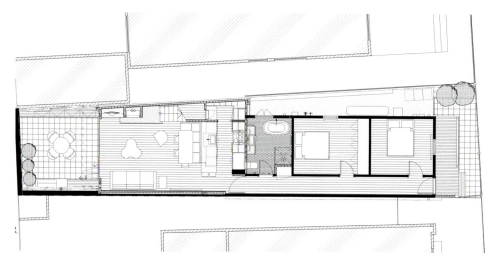

First-floor plan

PICTURE FRAME HOUSE

Location:
London, United Kingdom

Area:
1,076 square feet (100 square meters)

Completion:
2017

Design:
Archer + Braun

Photography:
David Barbour

Picture Frame House is a modern refresh of a terraced house in the Albert Gardens Conservation Area of Stepney Green, East London. The house had not been updated since the 1970s and was in need of a revamp. The renovation enlarges the first floor with a side infill extension and rearranges it to allow for a larger flexible kitchen area.

The interior is also fully refurbished and enhanced through a playful, creative design and custom-made accent elements that give the home a unique contemporary character.

The designers collaborated with a local picture framer to fabricate bespoke American black walnut and oak "picture frames" to adorn different window-sized openings throughout the home. This aperture design tempers a fully open-plan layout to allow the kitchen, lounge, and dining area to be defined without merging into one another. It also creates opportunities for unexpected interactions between the inhabitants.

The once dark and unused dining room now has a view into the kitchen—fitted with an Ikea "hack" kitchen— and the garden beyond. A large skylight floods the kitchen with natural daylight throughout the day, creating an inviting space for meal preparations. Other feature accents include a bespoke oak tray frame mirror, Carrara marble elements, a book-matched mitred marble shower wall, flush tiled mosaic details, and custom-fit joinery in the kitchen and bedroom.

Smooth dark-gray bricks with flush color-matched mortar dress the exterior of the extension in a modern look. The outfit is completed with a window in a dark-gray polyester powder-coated "picture frame" to match the brickwork. The extension is designed to be similar in material to the existing envelope, but in a contrasting color, to read as a contemporary addition to the period property.

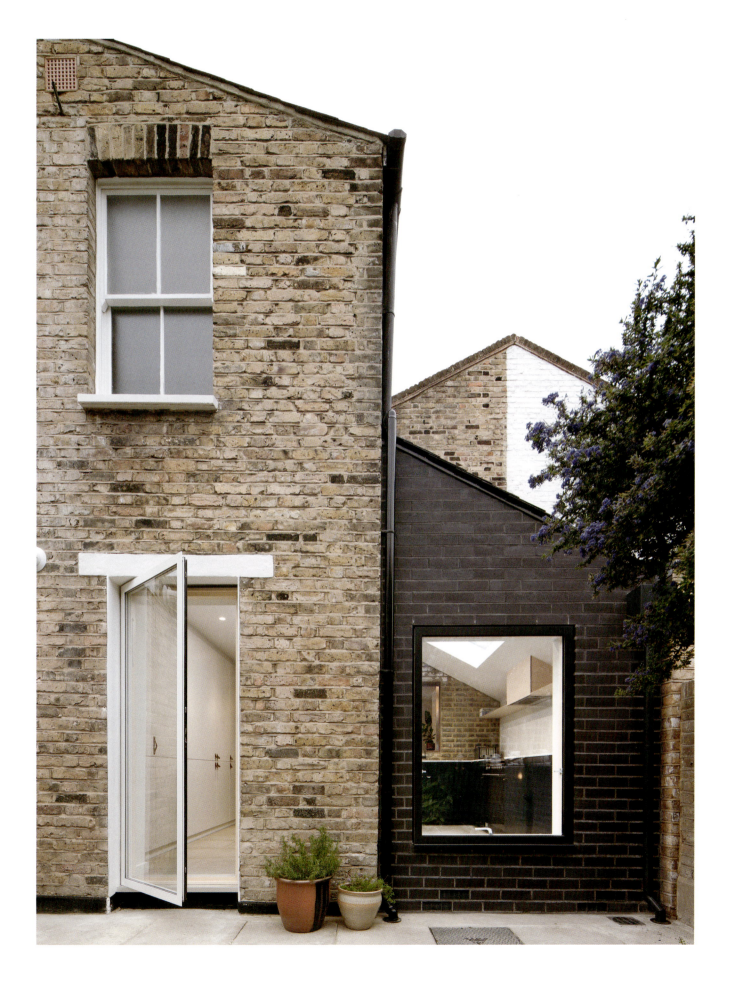

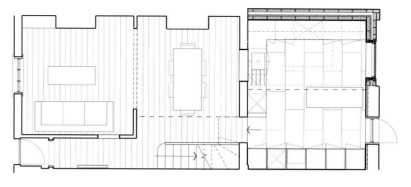

First-floor plan

Second-floor plan

FK HOUSE

Location:
São Paulo, Brazil
Area:
1,722 square feet (160 square meters)
Completion:
2018
Design:
COA Associados
Photography:
Pedro Vannucchi

The homeowners, who live in the house with their two children, sought to adapt their home to their lifestyle with a renovation that would converse with the existing construction, and which would tailor an environment that speaks to them.

Their main requests were to improve lighting and ventilation in the social areas on the first floor by integrating the spaces, and for the indoor environment to weave a strong relationship with the outside. To that end, a toy room is transformed into a backyard with a deck, and the garage into a front garden. The kitchen, living room, dining room, and outdoor spaces on the first floor are integrated and organized around a core that locates the stairs and toilet, to deliver a broader, more socially effective use of the area. To achieve this integration of spaces, walls were removed, and new foundations and metallic structures were executed to change the structural logic of the building.

The plastic from the original brick wall is done away with and the wall is painted white to remember the old residence, and also to function as a conducive backdrop to display art and other loved personal items of the family. The warm tone of wood flooring in the bedrooms and other social areas ties the interior together to create a modern, yet homey ambiance.

Perforated metal sheet sunshades on the upper floor, in addition to concrete eaves that shade and serve as support for the landscaping, create more openings in the façades that facilitate a relationship between the internal and external spaces. Specific landscaping in the periphery lends the uplifting vibrance of greenery to the interior of the home, creating a light, cheerful atmosphere. At the entrance, the vegetation shields the interface from the street; at the back, it surrounds the office and offers calm seclusion; and on the social deck, it appears in the form of small vegetable gardens near the kitchen.

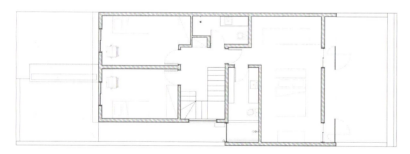

Second-floor plan

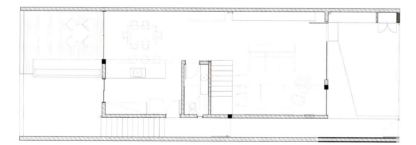

First-floor plan

071

HILLSIDE MIDCENTURY

Location:
Seattle, Washington, United States
Area:
2,250 square feet (209 square meters)
Completion:
2017
Design:
SHED Architecture & Design
Photography:
Rafael Soldi

Hillside Midcentury is a redesigned 1957 architect-designed home in the heart of Seattle that restores the home's midcentury elements to their original intent, while also integrating modern details.

The two floors of the home were originally mirrored—a common architectural approach in the 1950s—so, instead of implementing major structural changes, the new design updates the kitchen, bathrooms, and bedrooms to better align the spaces with the family's living patterns.

On the main floor, the unifying strut provides lateral strength and a datum line that organizes different passageways from the entry to the kitchen. To introduce color highlights, as requested by the homeowners, the kitchen is updated with cabinets in a maroon laminate from Beech Tree Woodworks. The flooring is replaced in most parts of the home, except in the dining and living rooms, where the original hardwood floors are retained, along with the green slate floor at the entry.

The main suite, originally two bedrooms, is modified by transforming one of the bedrooms into a main bath that features a floating vanity and open shower. To meet the homeowners' request for a powder room on the main floor and overcome the space limitation, a separate toilet compartment, off the master bath, is designed, serving both functions.

The first-floor entry from the garage is modified and a dedicated mud room is incorporated using a wood screen (designed in-house), to separate the flex space from the entry without inhibiting light. The homeowners also wanted a pool added, which was a challenge in the small footprint of the site. To meet the request, an old tool shed is transformed into a pool for cooling splashes in summer.

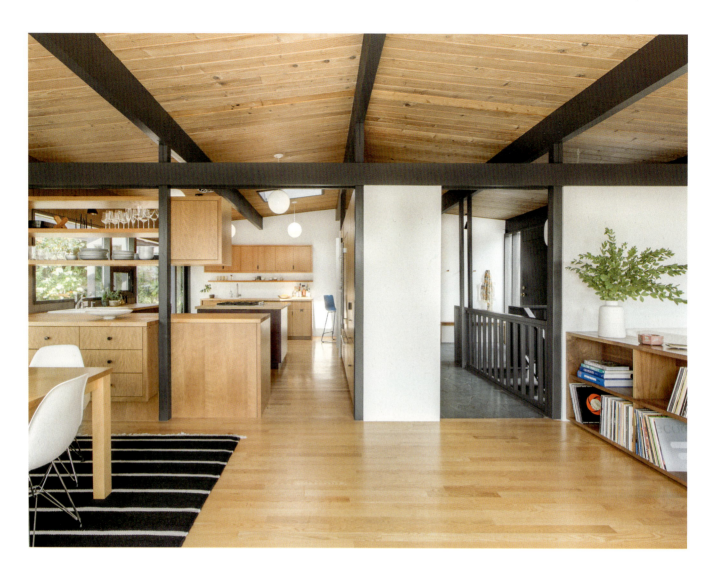

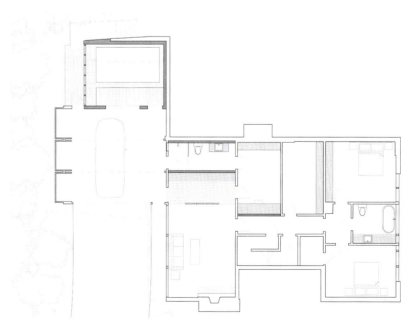

Floor plan

LIGHT FALLS

Location:
London, United Kingdom
Area:
3,122 square feet (290 square meters)
Completion:
2019
Design:
FLOW Architecture in partnership with Magrits
Photography:
NAARO

This Victorian terraced house on a tree-lined street in Kensington has been redeveloped with an almost complete demolition and reconstruction of the existing dwelling, a four-story end-of-terrace house originally built in 1851. A basement and a double-height rear extension are also added.

The homeowners sought to address the traditional compartmentalized Victorian layout (usual in such historical housing) and the poor quality of light inside the home in the revamp. Based on that, spatial planning is driven by maximizing natural light in the home and the fluidity of the vertically stacked living spaces to accommodate the owners' lifestyles.

As the external appearance of the house had to be preserved—as it is within the Abingdon Conservation Area and subject to planning restrictions—the redesign is concentrated around the core of the building. A new interior courtyard reorganizes the plan and performs as a visual center of the living spaces. Next to the courtyard, a series of double-height spaces amplify the effect of the cross-views throughout the living quarters, and a staircase opens toward the bottom section of the house to arrange a sequence of entertainment areas.

To drench the home in natural light, two large, frameless skylights are positioned at the top of the courtyard and the open staircase; they also enhance the permeability of the building. The abundant daylight that cascades in and fills the heart of the dwelling carves out the volumes from the original mass, creating a series of fascinating effects.

Natural light and visual connections are extended further with the glass rear extension. With this, the dining room enjoys a direct visual link to the garden. Sliding panels open to a generous terrace that greets a large walnut tree. The walls here are cladded in glassfiber-reinforced-concrete (GRC) panels that fold out to form a curved bench and the stairs to the garden, reflecting the dynamic lines of the sculptural interior treatment.

The strong visual connections around and beyond the home, married with the changing hues of light on whitewashed walls, create a light, uplifting atmosphere, as a bespoke décor and creative interior design tailor a space of contemporary comfort.

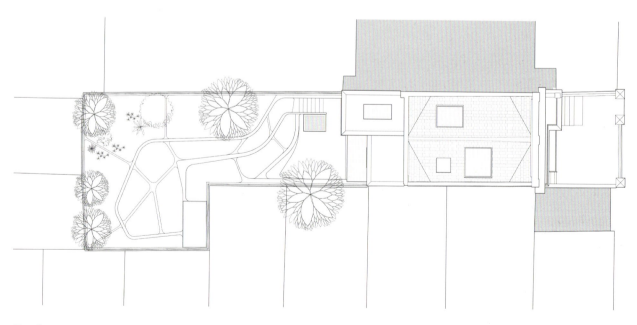

Site plan

Second-floor plan

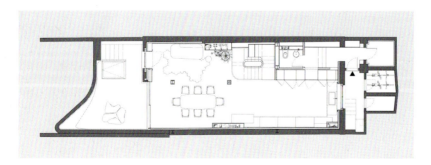

First-floor plan

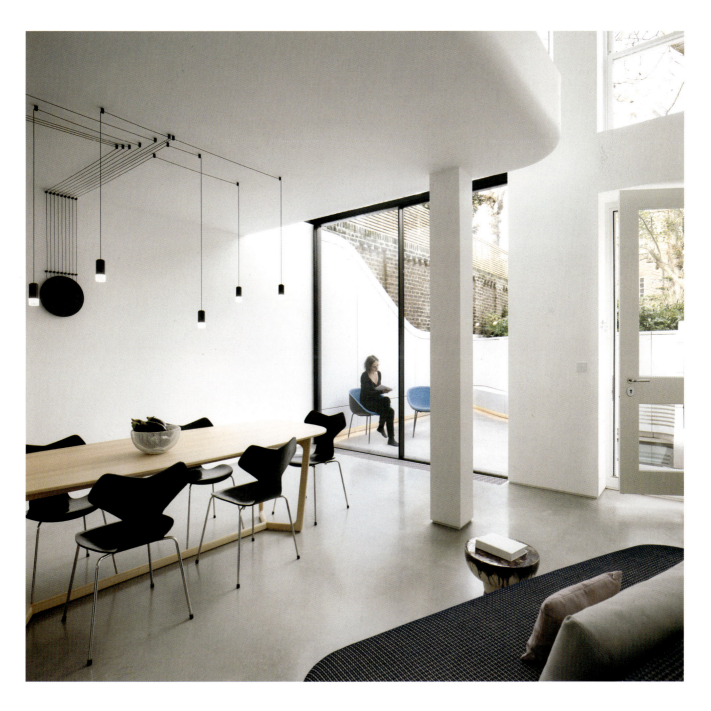

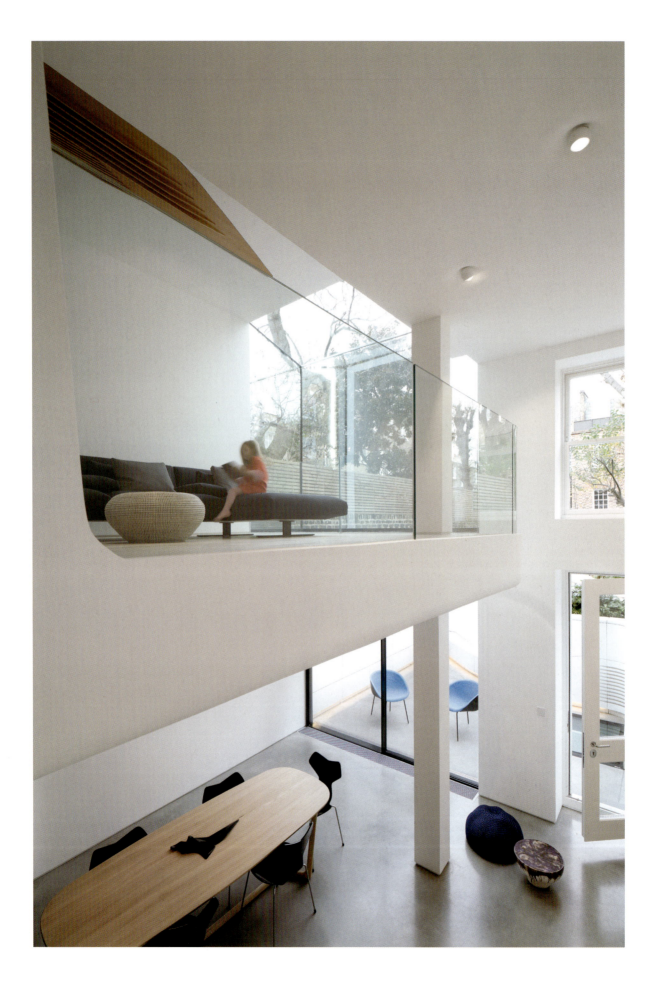

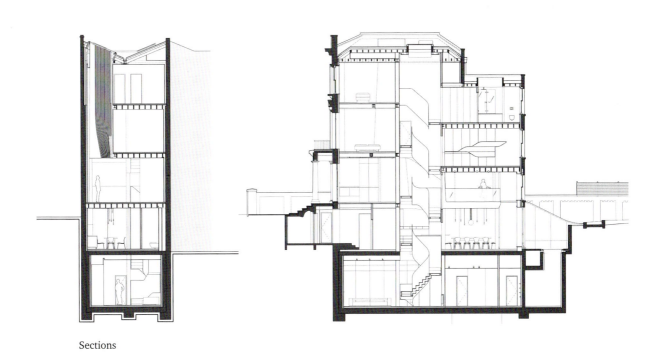

Sections

MIBUNAKAGAWA HOUSE

Location:
Kyoto, Japan
Area:
1,071 square feet (100 square meters)
Completion:
2020
Design:
Alts Design Office
Photography:
Kenta Kawamura

This generations-old private house in Kyoto has a narrow frontage (like most homes in the city), therefore, strict building coverage and floor-area ratio decided a renovation instead of a rebuild as the most effective course of revamp.

Previous remodeling works had resulted in a dark living space on the first floor; the redesign combines floors of various heights, and arranges a bedroom, bathroom, and a living, dining, and kitchen area, and ingeniously uses the way light flows in the home to maximize the space and create a sense of openness, so that it does not feel confined and limited. By creating a compact and neat space that does not require brightness, the bedroom, living room, dining room, and kitchen are opened up and reawakened.

As the building may have been built on the borderline of the site, a staircase facing the road is added to the design to extend the distance between passersby moving along on the sidewalk and the home's living space. The staircase also doubles as a lightwell that casts light into the interior.

Various functions and uses of the space is enabled by setting the landing of the staircase different from the floor heights.

A wall is set up to secure the space only around the bathroom, where privacy is required. This creates a distinct segregation in the home's areas, also defining a separation in its aesthetic atmospheres, such as a "warm" space and a "cool" space.

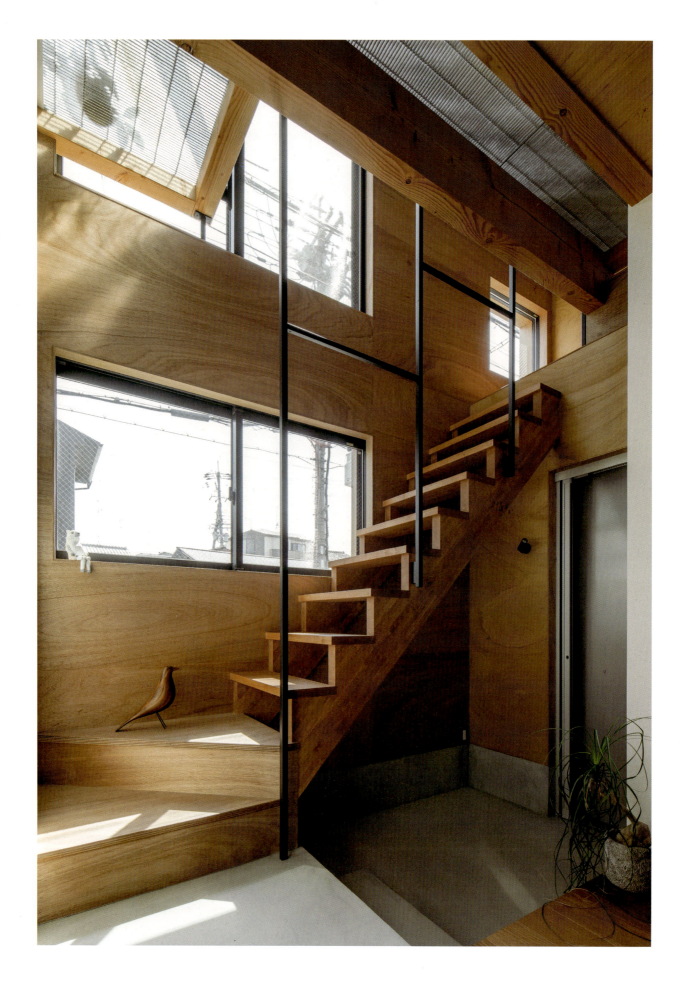

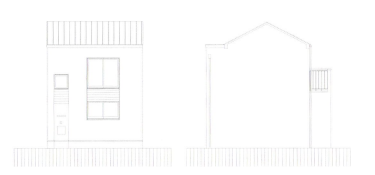

Elevations

Section

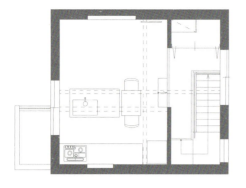

Second-floor plan

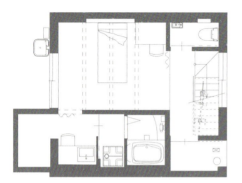

First-floor plan

SHANGHAI XUHUI OLD HOUSE RENOVATION AND INTERIOR DESIGN

Location:
Shanghai, China
Area:
2,153 square feet (200 square meters)
Completion:
2019
Design:
Nong Studio
Photography:
Chasing Wang

The design of this old mansion in the former French Concession area takes inspiration from the mixed ethnicity and heritage of the homeowner couple, who are a Chinese husband and a European wife.

The house is a brick/wood entity that is more than fifty years old, and in honor of that, the renovation works were conscientiously tailored to respect its history. On this premise, the suspended ceiling was removed to carefully restore the original wood structure. Fully utilizing the home's original 23-foot (7-meter) floor height, a mezzanine, floor-to-ceiling windows, and eave-opening skylights were installed, not only satisfying the client's brief, but also enhancing air circulation and allowing better views of the scenery outside.

The interior is divided into private and public, and dynamic and quiet areas. Beginning from the foyer, the left side marks the private area and the right side the public. The main suite on the left side contains a bedroom, bathroom, built-in wardrobe, and balcony on the second floor, and arranges a walk-in closet on the mezzanine. The wall partition on the right side is removed to allow the space to flow freely; an open-plan kitchen connects with the living area, while a tearoom, yoga space, terrace, guest room, and storage find space on the mezzanine.

Modern lines, white walls, and a wood floor tailor a clean and pure décor in the interior that exudes calm and peace. A black metal fireplace in the center of the living room sets the stage for cozy gatherings and chit-chat with friends around a warm fire. An eclectic assembly of old, new, and Western and Eastern furnishings and decorations, as well as souvenirs and collectibles from the couple's travels to faraway exotic destinations—which include tapestries from Chile, porch cabinets from Morocco, utensils from Thailand, and wood carvings from Africa—beautifies the home with colors and a spirit that sings passionately of life.

Window system

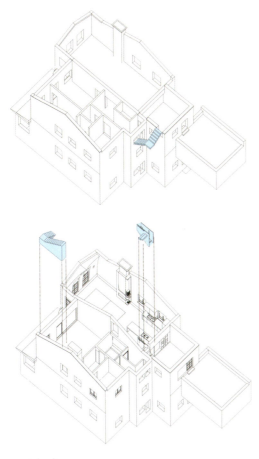

Axonometric view

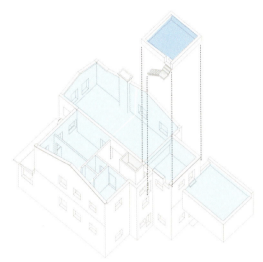

Before

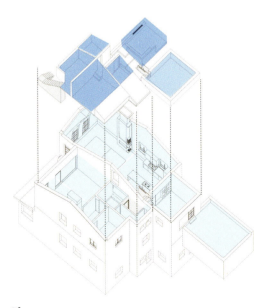

After

Second-floor plan

First-floor plan

THE JOURNEY HOUSE

Location:
Melbourne, Australia
Area:
1,830 square feet (170 square meters)
Completion:
2015
Design:
Nic Owen Architects
Photography:
Christine Francis

The homeowners' wish list highlighted more space, updated amenities, a strong connection to the outside, and a tranquil and relaxing environment to call home. A renovation and rear extension that retains the original building transform this 1940s semi-detected clinker-brick house, adding modern life to a tired midcentury classic to deliver the brief.

The property sits on a generous allotment; a clever design conceals the modern extension and presents the home as its old clinker-brick self. As one enters and journeys through, the home introduces its modern updates.

The existing hallway directs the plan through a curved, black-timber-clad passage that hides the end from sight, planning the destination as a surprise. Coming out of the passage, a large timber "encasing" emerges into view, framing the new, open-plan living area that explores outward to finish in a timber deck on the outside. An acutely angled ceiling delivers a sloping overhead that creates a tent-like feeling. An intersection of glass and timber, the new extension is orientated to the north and wrapped in a monolithic external skin that respects the character of the existing neighborhood.

The single-vaulted roof line rises up to the north, providing a feeling of space, while still maintaining an intimate human scale. The increased vertical height fits the space with high windows that capture extended views of neighboring trees. This generous glazing also allows abundant natural light to fill the space, creating a cheery ambiance to backdrop home activities.

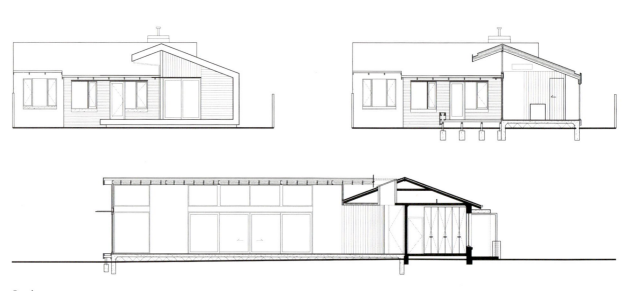

Sections

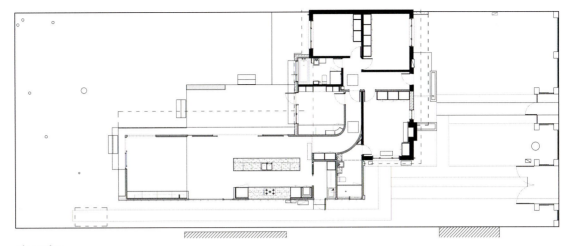

Floor plan

BEIRA MAR HOUSE

Location:
Aveiro, Portugal

Area:
1,410 square feet (131 square meters)

Completion:
2018

Design:
Paulo Martins Arquitectura & Design

Photography:
Ivo Tavares Studio

Located in one of the most typical and established neighborhoods of Aveiro (Beira Mar), this residence is the result of a passionate and challenging renovation. The main intention strives to give the homeowners contact with outdoor spaces—the sound of seagulls and the smell of the sea breeze; the color of the sky and the green of the vegetation—as well as a sense of freedom in lifestyle.

Built on a plot of land that is 98 feet (30 meters) long and 8 feet (2.5 meters) wide, the property formally establishes itself as a habitable corridor. Right from the entry, it takes one through moments of darkness, light, surprise, discovery, compression, and finally release, at the back-yard patio.

Basic and essential functions—such as the floor and the space that houses the bathrooms and service area—are designed in sober and elemental materials like concrete. The building has been covered and protected with plasterboard painted dark green to rigorously shield it in its new life cycle.

By conceptual and practical contrast to the dark, intimate interior environment, the exterior is white, as a purposefully reflective surface, to flood the house with light—sometimes diffused and soft, sometimes direct and intense.

All social functions are planned on the first floor, in direct contact with the house's backyard patio, while the upper floor is reserved for bedrooms and a solarium, visually concealed by a plant curtain.

This home is designed to be lived in and experienced in the privacy and freshness of the exterior, aware and accepting of the past, but with an open, respectful anticipation of the future.

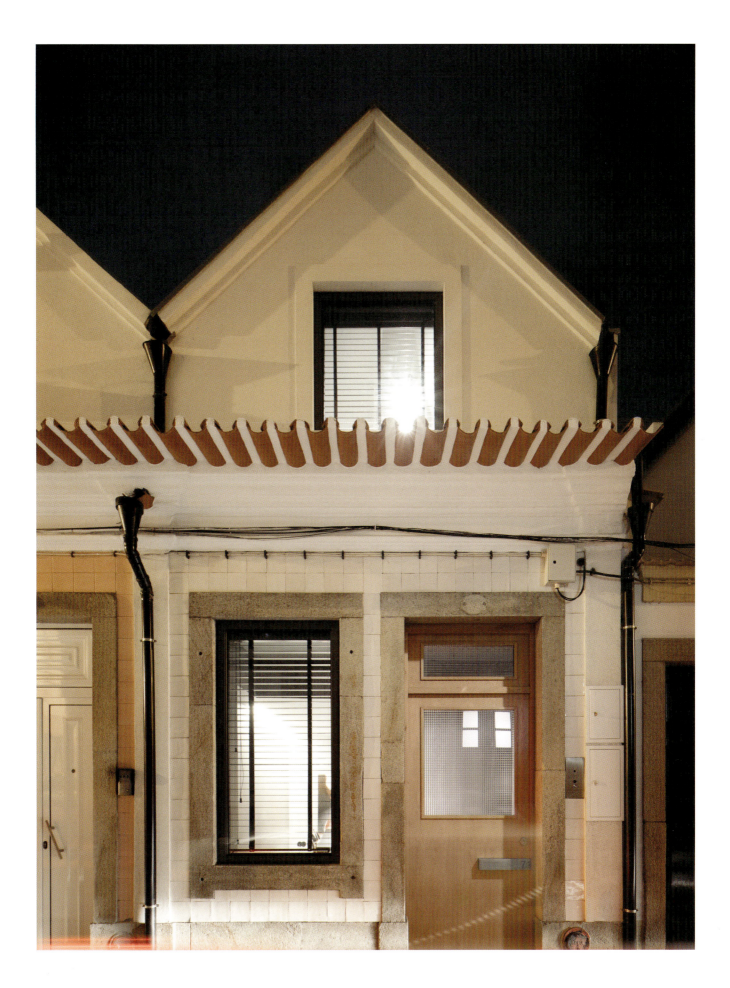

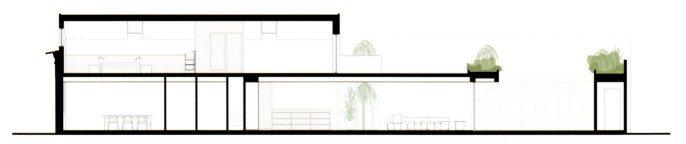

Section

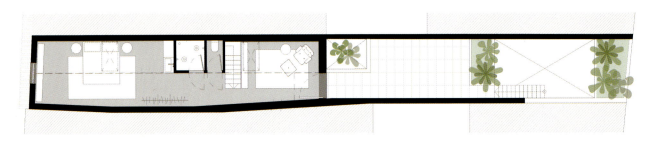

Second-floor plan

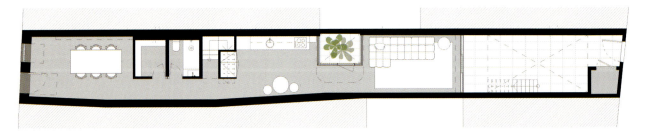

First-floor plan

HOUSE BETWEEN PILLARS

Location:
Tokyo, Japan
Area:
1,281 square feet (119 square meters)
Completion:
2016
Design:
Yusuke Fujita, Naoko Aramaki | Camp Design Inc.
Photography:
Kenta Hasegawa

This renovation project redesigns an empty home to renew its market value in order to sell it. The concept of the renovation assumes a hypothetical family in their 30s to 40s, with children, as the homeowners, and designs the remodeling to fit the lifestyle of such homeowners.

The overarching tone of the redesign is a versatile and variable dwelling. Traditional Japanese wooden frameworks consist of modules with pillar spacings of 72 inches (1.8 meters). Fittings are installed between most of the pillars, and with the fittings tailored to the module, the new homeowners can define flexible boundaries that can be easily altered.

The architects also designed an interesting space coined as "Between the Pillars." This space goes through the center to the first and second floors and becomes an intermediate area when changing the plan (by way of moving the joiners) to format different layouts. In addition to this, movable furniture is also designed according to the module, and it becomes an element that sets with the fittings.

The property now becomes an "old" new house that changes shape according to changes in lifestyle and the size of the family—made possible by the traditional Japanese wooden framework standards and the fittings method. This structural format can be applied universally, serving as a tool to fix the formal characteristics of wooden frames to accommodate the flow of changes that take place in the family's lifestyle over time. By drawing on the flexibility of the unit of such forms and tools, it is possible to create updates in wooden frameworks and even incorporate urban design aspects.

After one year　　　　　　　　　After fifteen years　　　　　　　　After thirty years

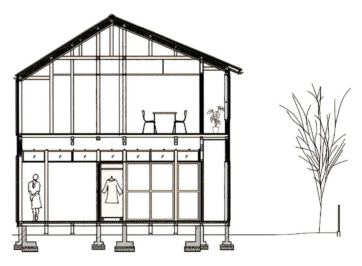

Section

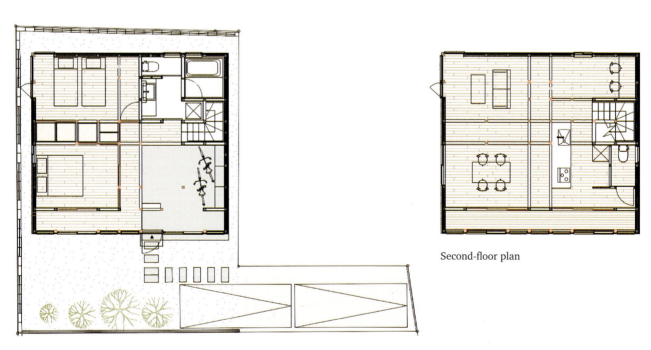

First-floor plan

Second-floor plan

RESIDENCE FOR BIJU MATHEW

Location:
Kerala, India
Area:
1,345 square feet (125 square meters)
Completion:
2016
Design:
Zero Studio
Photography:
Ar Prasanth Mohan

The client wanted a small home for his family of three (himself—a teacher—his wife, and their two-year-old son), and he also wanted the house to "look small," and be simple but elegant, with no ornamental detailing or a massive form. Though it would have been more convenient and sensible to design a new home to realize the aspirations of the client, the "reinvention" of the existing home became the course of the project, encouraged by the architect's belief that unconventional choices sometimes create remarkable outcomes.

The project's main constraints were formed by the "hostility" of the spaces; they were not a match for the client's requirements (the brief was for a simple and graceful home for a small family) and were, to an extent, aesthetically unappealing.

The site, too, brought its own challenges. It is small, and located by the side of a narrow road in a residential area, and there was no provision for an elaborate front yard. Thus, breaking the verticality was crucial.

The emphasis on horizontal lines, thereby camouflaging the height of the site, is achieved with a car porch to the right and designing no openings or windows in the façade. Only the entrance with a sit-out space breaches this intentional enclosure. The rest of the façade remains faithful to the idea of horizontality through a screen of equally spaced metal pipes.

The interior spaces are reinvented by removing unwanted walls and bringing in natural light and ventilation to make the home energy efficient. The main aspects of sustainability lie in the reuse of materials, the thermal comfort attained, and the overall energy efficiency.

Lightwells and a double-layered roof enhance thermal comfort and the flow of light, so that interior spaces are well lit and adequately ventilated, even without windows opening to the elevations. The décor speaks plainly and directly with pale-colored walls, wooden flooring, and a selection of furnishings that make no bold statements to maintain a calm, cohesive, and restorative environment.

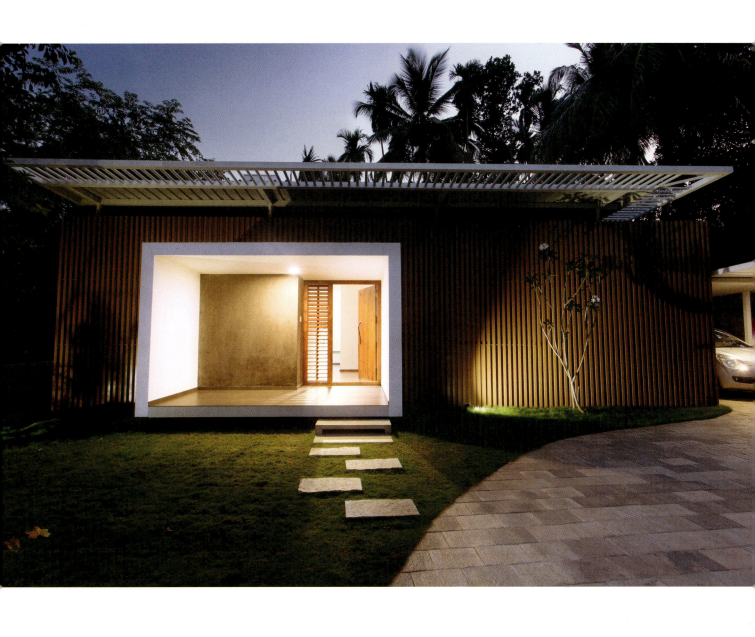

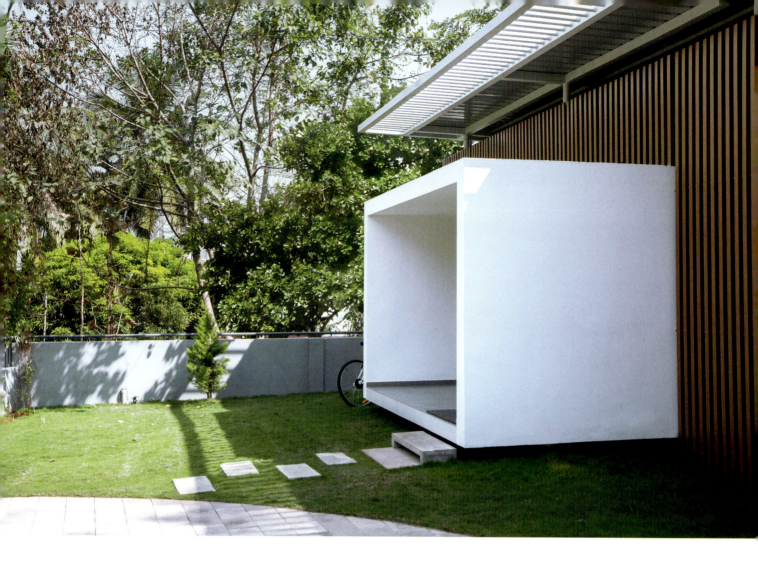

An additional floor has been added in the renovation to be used as multifunctional space, but it remains elusive until one chances upon the stairs that lead up to it. The focus on horizontality makes this illusion possible, together with the minimal façade and the exterior landscape that blends into it.

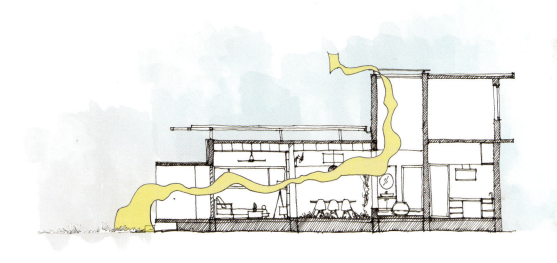

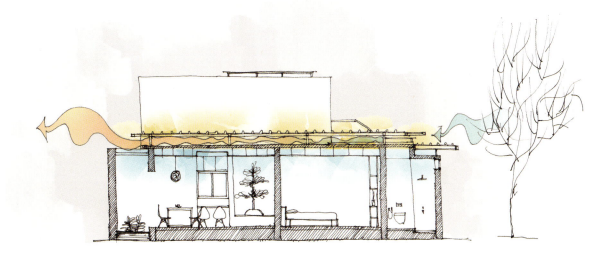

Sections

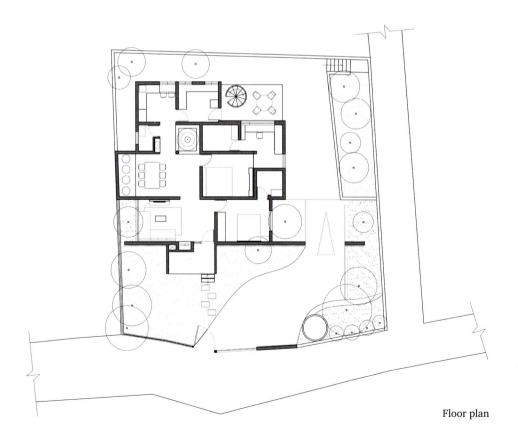

Floor plan

RAERAE HOUSE

Location:
Melbourne, Australia
Area:
3,993 square feet (371 square meters)
Completion:
2020
Design:
Austin Maynard Architects
Photography:
Peter Bennetts

The homeowners had been preparing to renovate and extend their tired single-fronted terrace in North Fitzroy, Melbourne. Just then, the house next door came up for sale; they decided to purchase the property and remodel both units to create a family home for life, for their clique of five. RaeRae House is a new five-bedroom that incorporates the front of two pre-existing heritage building terrace homes. A glazed entry that is set back between the buildings unites the two home fronts and forms the gateway to the new house.

The two terraces are each sited on long blocks that have dual frontage potential, a street at the front, and an unusually wide lane at the rear. The newly purchased home was dilapidated and in an unlivable condition. Squatters had been using the premises and had even torn off floorboards for firewood. The home was structurally unsound and needed to be demolished. However, a heritage overlay dictates that the street frontages of both homes must remain, so the architects combined the neighboring properties to design a single home with a garden and generous outdoor area.

The design opens to the wide laneway at the rear scaped by garages, home extensions, subdivisions, and newer builds that have capitalized on the dual frontage aspect. With no heritage constraints on this frontage, the house is able to engage with the street and neighbors, with direct access, large openings, and windows. Factoring in possible future changes in the family's transportation needs, the garage is designed as a multifunctional space that is fully insulated to allow for future use as an extra bedroom or rental unit.

On the interior layout, things unfold slightly unusually. Instead of the often-requested quiet parental retreat away from active family areas, the owners desired the main bedroom to, unconventionally, be at the very center of the house. With the main bedroom placed directly above the kitchen, they can directly engage with the activity below, and when privacy is needed, large sliding doors close to create a contained space.

The children also have their own versatile areas. The rumpus room opens out to the garden and also to the street, and is future-proofed to become self-contained with its own direct street access. At the back is a dedicated craft/study area that can double as a creative studio for artistic messes, and as a secluded nook for quiet revision.

The home is specifically built along the southern boundary to take full advantage of the northern aspect. Living spaces greet the sunny northern garden, while storage and services are tucked in the south. This reorienting along the southern boundary not only maximizes passive solar gain, it also presents a sunny garden with minimal shadow.

All windows are double-glazed with fixed external awnings that provide shade. A combination of thoughtful design and sustainable systems maximize available daylight and optimize passive solar gain in winter, while also ensuring that the summer sun is not felt too harshly.

The effective management of shade and passive ventilation substantially reduces the demands on mechanical heating and cooling. A large water tank buried within the garden collects roof water for reuse in the flushing system and garden irrigation. The house is designed to be durable and long-lasting: slate roofing offers a highly robust surface that comes with an extended life span at little to no maintenance. The plus: slate is a natural material derived simply from the earth without undergoing an environmentally harming manufacturing process; it is chemical deficient and can be unattached and reused, continuously reviving its life cycle.

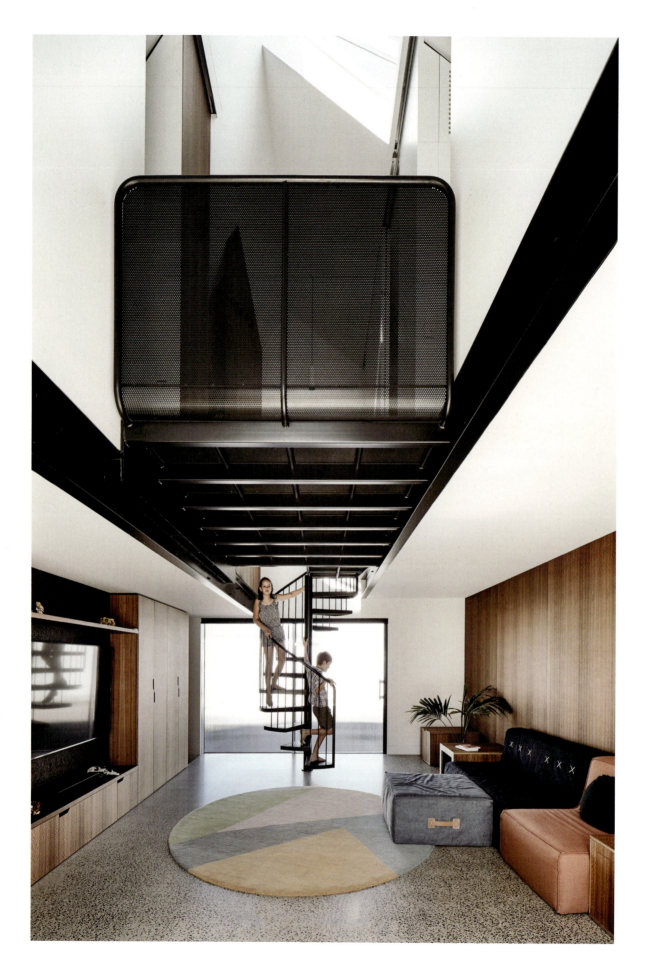

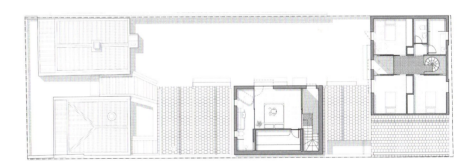

Second-floor plan

First-floor plan

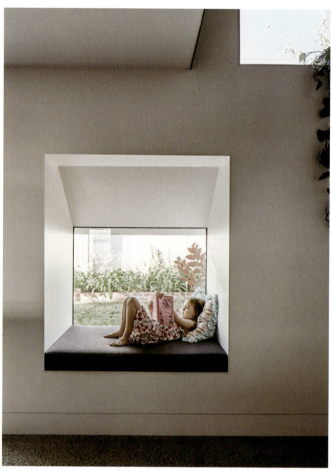

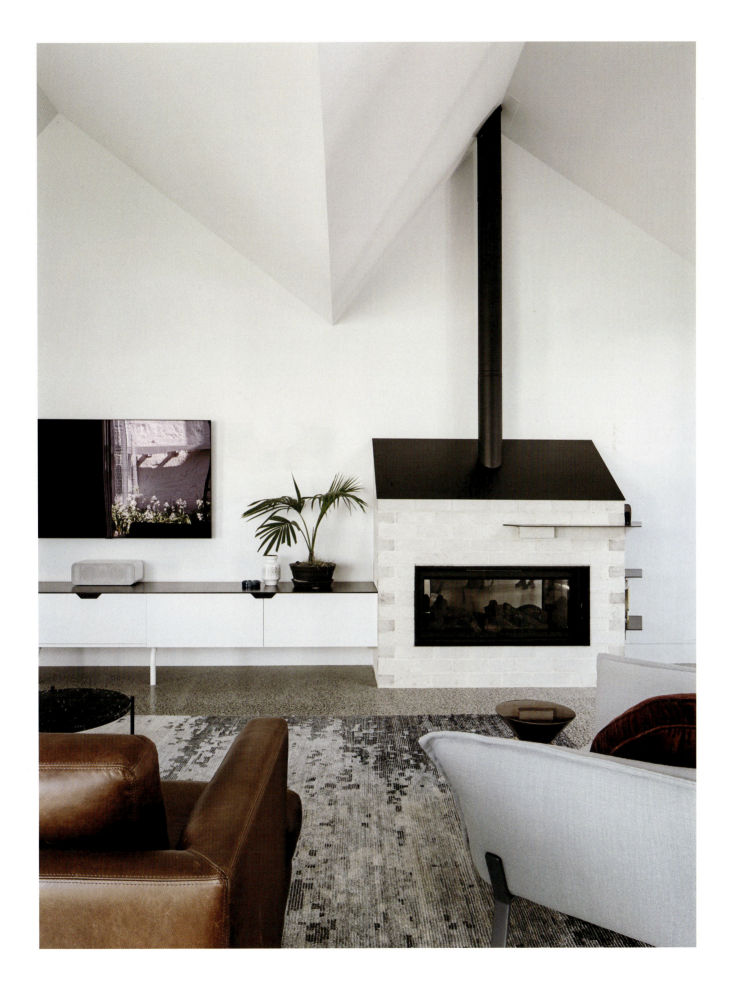

MAISONETTE IN NOTTING HILL

Location:
London, United Kingdom
Area:
1,071 square feet (100 square meters)
Completion:
2019
Design:
Francesco Pierazzi Architects
Photography:
Lorenzo Zandri

This is a remodel of a recently acquired maisonette to improve the neglected interior and convert an existing steep roof space into an additional living accommodation.

The challenge: create an original story to inform the interiors—which would now span three levels—without the possibility of bold architectural interventions to the terrace, while also concurrently maximizing the internal floor area.

The design approach adopts a strategy inspired by French philosopher Maurice Merleau-Ponty, who stressed that the body is the primary site of knowing the world (in opposition to the more traditional approach that states that consciousness is the informant of knowledge). The rejuvenated interior composition is tasked to stimulate the bodies of the inhabitants as they negotiate different spaces in the house, be it when ascending or descending, so that daily activities and movements within and around the maisonette become an enhanced choreography that transforms static spaces into dynamic experiences.

The middle floor is reconfigured to reduce circulation space in favour of larger bedrooms and service facilities, and the brick shell of the house is treated as a blank volume. The stairwell is designed as a subordinate space within a primary volume and lined with birch plywood from the first floor to the roof level. In other areas, the seamless gray floors and white vertical surfaces are reduced and kept to the minimum, so as to allow the organic character and natural beauty of the timber in the interior to come through.

To create interest across the three floors against the mild interior palette, contrasting materials are selected for specific areas and juxtaposed against each other to create tensions between precious, semi-precious, and off-the-shelf materials.

For example, gray vinyl tiles contrast with ordinary whitewashed bricks, birch plywood panels, cast-iron radiators, and precious marbles. The existing envelope was central to the design strategy, informing the concept every step of the way, almost as if the house was designing itself, dressing to embrace its new lease on life.

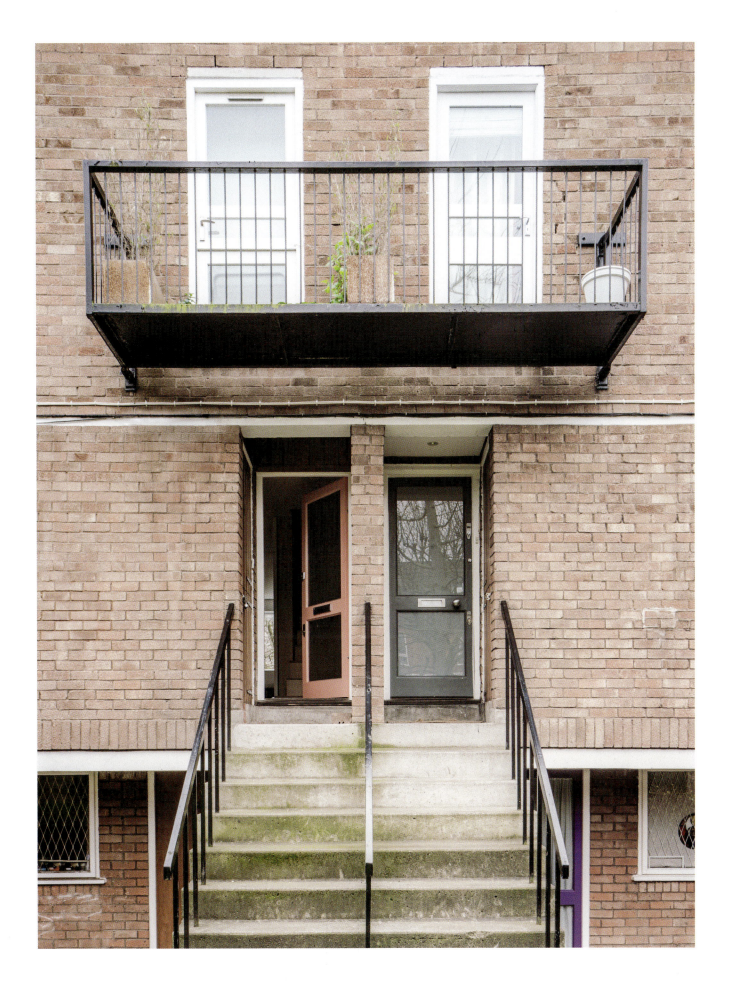

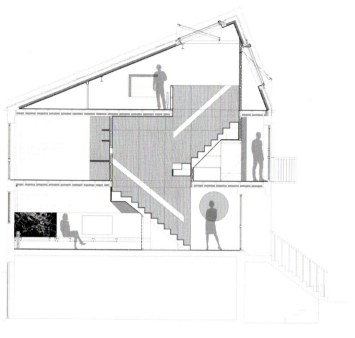

Section

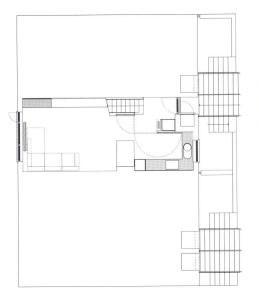 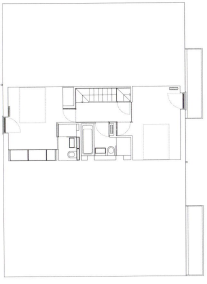 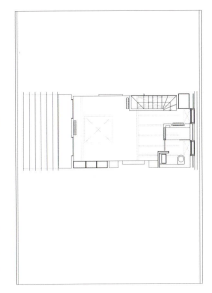

First-floor plan Second-floor plan Third-floor plan

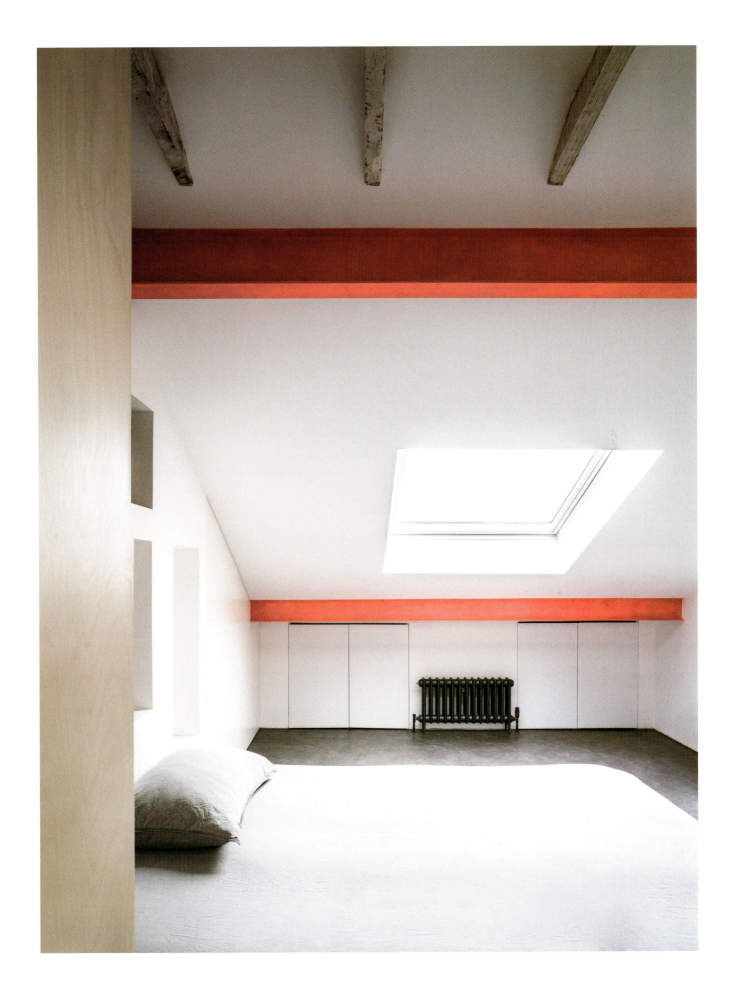

HOUSE C

Location:
Léchelles, Switzerland

Area:
484 square feet (45 square meters)

Completion:
2018

Design:
Studio 17 architectes

Photography:
Dylan Perrenoud

Some houses, like House C, are built without specific considerations of their surroundings; like a foreign edifice "plonked" into the middle of a plot. A suburban villa in the countryside of Fribourg, the house was closed on itself, alarmingly rejecting the beautiful green landscape of its surroundings, large openings to nature, and its position at the end of the village; it was also very distant from its garden.

In this extension project, the additional construction is a very precise device that reorientates the house, turns it, and opens it to its wonderful garden. The space is organized in sequences, in accordance with, and open to its surroundings.

The extension huddles to the house and is faithful to its limits, but with a sensual twist. The construction is simple, yet sophisticated. The consisting elements can be simplified into three main parts: a concrete base that negotiates with the topography and the diverse accesses to the house; a continuous glass layer that allows a panoramic view of the landscape; and a light roof supported by slender galvanized columns.

The roof elaborates the continuity of the existing ceramic covering, but in its own lingo, iterating the covering in a different material (visible gray bitumen) and geometry (sharp angles and cut sides). Each of those elements has an applicable logic: first model the surroundings, then adapt to the existing house.

The expression of the extension is simple, avoiding superfluous elements to present a straightforward appearance, but without losing its radicality and delicacy. Inside, the plan extends the common living areas of the existing house. The overall footprint measures 484 square feet (45 square meters) and feels comfortable, thanks to the spatial split with the level difference that allows a direct connection to the outside. The resulting inner space becomes a realm of continuity between the house and the garden, enjoying uplifting views of nature and the vastness of the open landscape.

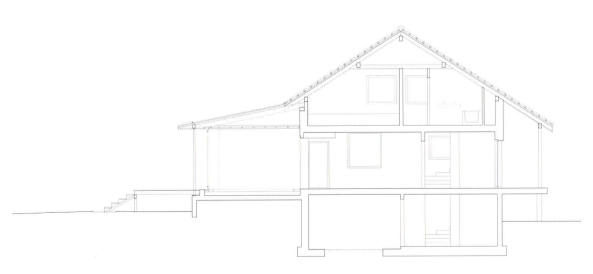

Section

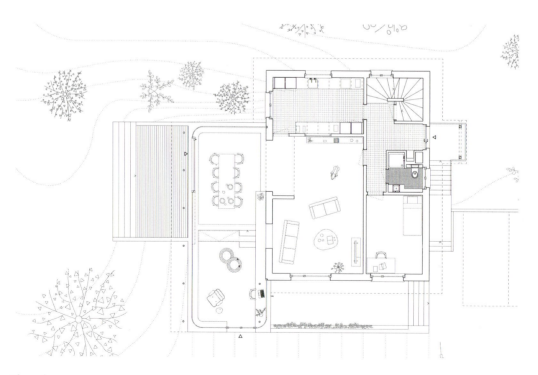

Floor plan

HOUSE IN HANEGI

Location:
Tokyo, Japan

Area:
1,636 square feet (152 square meters)

Completion:
2019

Design:
Yusuke Fujita | Camp Design Inc.

Photography:
Kenta Hasegawa

This minimalist residence in Hanegi sits close to the main road in a quiet residential area. The greater landscape is a tapestry of abundant natural greenery—contributed by a pocket of old forest that has been preserved— houses, and a condominium that has a tenant list that includes famous architects.

Given its dense surroundings of neighboring houses, ensuring privacy within the home was one of the focal points, along with establishing a continuity with its neighborhood on the exterior. Other design modifications to update the plan were beyond consideration due to the challenging structural arrangement of the house—the first floor of the existing building had a bearing wall that divides the space, and the second floor was a section with a central wall and beams.

The exterior appearance of the house was contemplated deeply, with the aim of giving it a distinct image, but still enable it to blend harmoniously with the townscape. The custom color palette of the exterior is derived by collecting color samples from the exteriors of the surrounding buildings, giving the house its own character, while allowing it to integrate with its surroundings and present itself as part of the townscape.

In addressing the point of privacy, the design also checks off daylight permeation in the interior, in the process, creating an identity statement on the exterior. Custom-made sliding window treatments in the same height as the interior walls keep the activities outside the home on the outside, to create a soft, cocooned ambiance in the inside. Referred to as *fusama* (usually functioning as sliding doors and walls in traditional Japanese homes), the screens are made of cloth and assembled with joinery. Against the windows, they become luminous lightboxes that define the essence of the interior. Their opaque translucence, almost ethereal, fill the space with comfortable, diffused light and add delicate, softly glowing ornamentation in the home, which complements the minimalistic décor. Seen from the outside, they interrupt the passive fluidity of the building face to arrange sheer apertures that contrast with the building's stony gray exterior, giving the house a distinct look. Other accents include

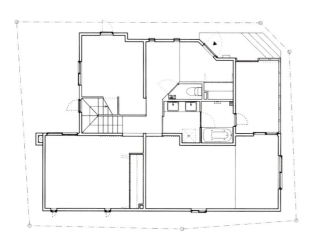

First-floor plan

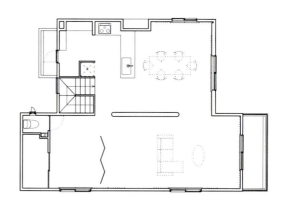

Second-floor plan

custom-made wooden doorknobs, lever handles, and knobs that enhance the texture of the entire house.

The plan of the main living area occurs around a large cement volume that divides the space while providing unrestricted flow through the various programs. A recessed area away from the main function connects the private terrace that links to the outdoor, making the space ideal as an alternative business or work area for home-run businesses.

HOUSE FOR FOUR GENERATIONS

Location:
Tokyo, Japan
Area:
1,493 square feet (139 square meters)
Completion:
2017
Design:
Tomomi Kito Architect & Associates
Photography:
Satoshi Shigeta

This interior renovation project redesigns a forty-year-old two-story timber-structure house in Tokyo for a four-generation family made up of a couple and their son, and the wife's parents and grandmother.

The clients (a young couple) had moved into the property to live with the wife's parents who were living there. Soon after, the wife's grandmother also decided to move into the house from the countryside and live together with her family. This created the need for a renovation to comfortably accommodate each of the four generations of the family and their varied personalities and preferences.

As the daily behavior and lifestyle patterns of each family member is different, the design approach was modeled on unity to create mutual shared spaces to promote connection between all generations in the house.

The existing rooms in the house were split into smaller functions and not open to the outside environment, nor to each other. This left the interior to struggle with a poor quality of natural light and ventilation; therefore, improving the quality of the space, and the flow of natural daylight and ventilation became essential.

The reorganized arrangement of the private areas takes full advantage of existing windows to maximize available natural light and ventilation. The remaining spaces are designated as "shared spaces" that are planned on each floor with utilities. They are consciously designed to connect with the outside—the entrance area on the first floor leads to the shared space, and a large window is installed in the shared space on the second floor overlooking the neighborhood—for two reasons. First: create channels for ventilation and opportunities for natural light to enter, so that family activities together in the shared spaces are conducted in an airy and uplifted atmosphere, rather than in a dingy, dim space. Second: the "shared" boundary between the outside and the inside symbolically iterates, as well as enhances, the concept of "share" in the shared space.

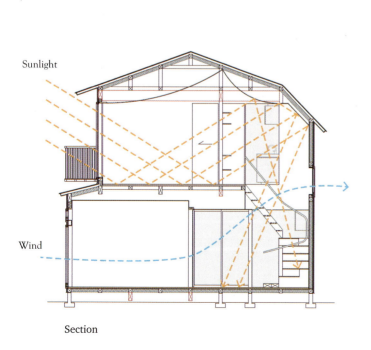

Sunlight

Wind

Section

The structure was also reviewed because it was discovered that the existing house was structurally unbalanced and lacked the necessary structural resistance, even though the columns were densely arranged in accordance with existing partitions. Reinforcements were added through supporting beams and structural plywood, while optimizing the use of the house's existing structural components. To that end, some columns were deemed redundant and removed, providing the opportunity to create more open spaces free of columns.

The ceiling of the shared space on the second floor is catenary shaped, allowing an organic connection to the outside, while maximizing the diffusion of natural light into the space. It also presents symbolically as a roof that lovingly shelters, and brings together under, it four generations of a family, within a home that protects and nurtures, and which will faithfully do so for many more generations to come.

Second-floor plan

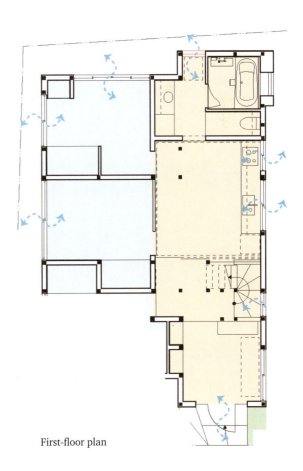

First-floor plan

CANDID HOUSE

Location:
Bangkok, Thailand
Area:
2,691 square feet (250 square meters)
Completion:
2018
Design:
INchan atelier Co., Ltd.
Photography:
Tharisra Chantip

This ten-year-old abandoned townhouse was renovated to be more than just a living space for a newly married couple in the photography profession. It also serves as a photoshoot studio and a photo gallery. The house is located in a good residential neighborhood in Bangkok; it has a good range of surrounding facilities and it is easy to get to downtown from the house, making it a viable investment for the young couple.

The existing structure was in overall good shape, but the building systems were not. There were leakage issues, bad electrical wiring, and poor sanitary networks. Adding to that, the quality of natural light was poor and the ventilation was insufficient, causing challenges in humidity control. Also, the original split-level organization of the house created rooms that were independent, and which could not be joined together.

The design concept designates the staircase and the walls along the stairs as the key attraction, which helps to also smoothly divide functional zones; the stairs detail intentionally catches attention and the walls are turned into a photo gallery. To maximize the volume of the rooms, most of the ceiling was removed, even if it meant exposing the pipes and wireways. Some façades were also redesigned, replacing existing walls, doors, and windows with new ones to introduce more natural light and ventilation into the building.

The parking space in front of the house has been turned into an outdoor gathering and relaxation area, with seating installed among greenery that include planters and trees in pots. The entrance level is designed to be the common floor for the house/office. It comprises a compact living space and a compact kitchen, where the dining table also performs as the kitchen island. The next level (the middle level) is split into two areas, according to the original structure, but with updates. The new design creates a livelier open well that also defines the border between public and private zones. This opening brings natural light and ventilation into the house that flow through the house through "interior windows" that also allow visual connection within the home.

As an example of a modern, compact home that serves a dual function—as a dwelling and a work space—Candid House is carefully crafted to reflect the owners' lifestyle in a signature design. It is an architectural solution to urban living that designs stylish work-live spaces within a compact footprint.

Section

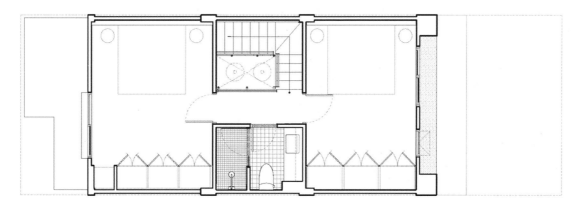

Third-floor plan

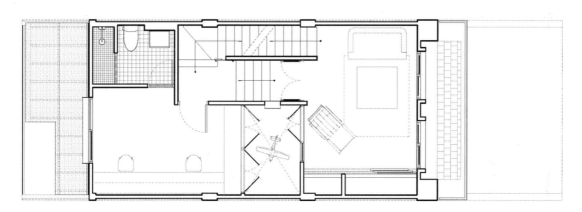

Second-floor plan

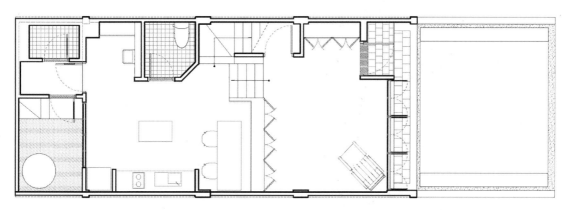

First-floor plan

HOUSE IN OYAMAZAKI

Location:

Kyoto, Japan

Area:

1,302 square feet (121 square meters)

Completion:

2020

Design:

Shimpei Oda Architect's Office, Atelier Loowe Inc.

Photography:

Norihito Yamauchi

The residential area in which the project is located was established in 1966 and was filled with a variety of terraced houses in the years that followed. This area played a major role in the development of Oyamazaki, with many of the buildings undergoing repeated renovations to gain extra floor area.

This house was one such frequently remodeled item that had collected a series of ambiguous rooms and corridors on its original plan, leaving the rooms in the center dark, without natural light. These continuous changes had, in a way, turned the house into a sort of migratory property, resulting in a peculiar plan.

The design concept uses this migratory nature to advantage, to negotiate the challenging structural load-bearing walls (usually in reinforced-concrete buildings such as this house) to plan an environment where the connection of spaces is linked in a continuous flow to be more "natural."

Empty pathways are eliminated by adding functions and the option to stay. This way, the various activities of everyday life that take place throughout the home integrate and connect the spaces; a resident moving around the house can be encouraged to settle down or perform different tasks in different places.

The garden, though unkempt and desolate from many years of neglect, contained a beautiful selection of firmly rooted trees and plants. A simple pruning and clean-up restored and revived it to become an outdoor oasis of calm for reflection and respite. It also guides natural light into the home, which gets further reflected into the rooms with walls painted white.

On the first floor, the walls of the staircase and the Japanese-style room are removed to relax the layout and connect the interior space more seamlessly, as well as brighten the ambiance. Replacing the second-floor wall with a *shoji* (a translucent, traditional Japanese screen) further enhances light flow in the stairwell. All in all, the home is transformed into a welcoming space that is inviting—with mainly timber finishes—and energized by natural light.

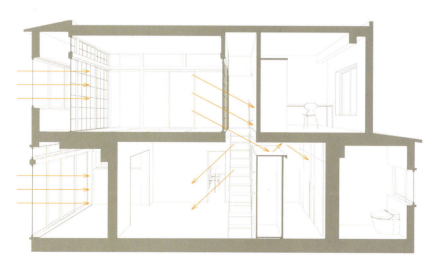

Section

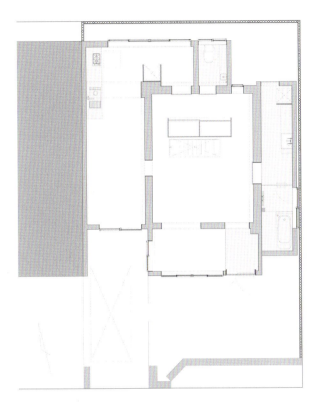

First-floor plan

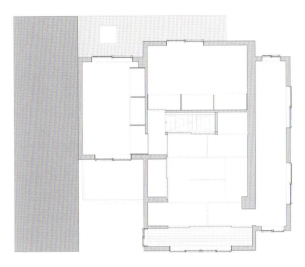

Second-floor plan

VILLA KURO

Location:
Joshua Tree, California, United States
Area:
1,991 square feet (185 square meters)
Completion:
2019
Design:
MINI INNO
Photography:
Stanley Yang Photography

Located in south Joshua Tree National Park, Villa Kuro is a midcentury ranch-style house that was originally built in the 1960s. Nestled in front of a boulder hill, the property extends all the way up to the peak of the mountain, framing beautiful nature at every turn. Tapping into the property's potential to offer a tranquil setting where one can slow down the fast pace of modern day, it was transformed into a contemporary, yet simple desert retreat that is away from the bustle, but not isolated from civilization.

Set in a quiet neighborhood, the single-story, two-bed, two-bath house sits on a 3.6-acre (1.45-hectare) site. Previous uncoordinated updates by more than one past owner had left the house in a state of mismatch, hence, the entire interior was stripped away to create a blank canvas and start fresh.

The gritty desert surroundings inspire a design concept that flows with the Japanese philosophy of *wabi sabi*, which is the outlook of finding beauty in imperfection and embracing it. Elements in the home are set with rustic hand-built techniques that speak to the origins of the house, as do other natural, reclaimed materials. Nothing lasts and nothing is perfect; as objects age, their patina and character emerge. This "deep" beauty is lost in shiny new objects. The previous lives of these reclaimed elements are honored, in the spirit of *wabi sabi*, by bringing out the textures of the wear they have endured. A neutral, pared-back interior lifts these subtle accents, while also enhancing the cues of the desert views that change through the day with the changing light.

The old garage, which occupied one of the best positions in the house, given its boulder mountain backdrop and views, is converted into a tearoom that can be used for relaxing, meditating, or simply recharging beside nature and enjoy watching wildlife that are out foraging.

Glass doors all around the house extend this connection with nature and the outdoors, along with outdoor living areas like a covered patio for dining, and a rock and cactus garden courtyard. Window seats invite a sit-down with a good book, while an outdoor shower, hot tub, and firepit add vivid colors to the experience of enjoying the outdoors.

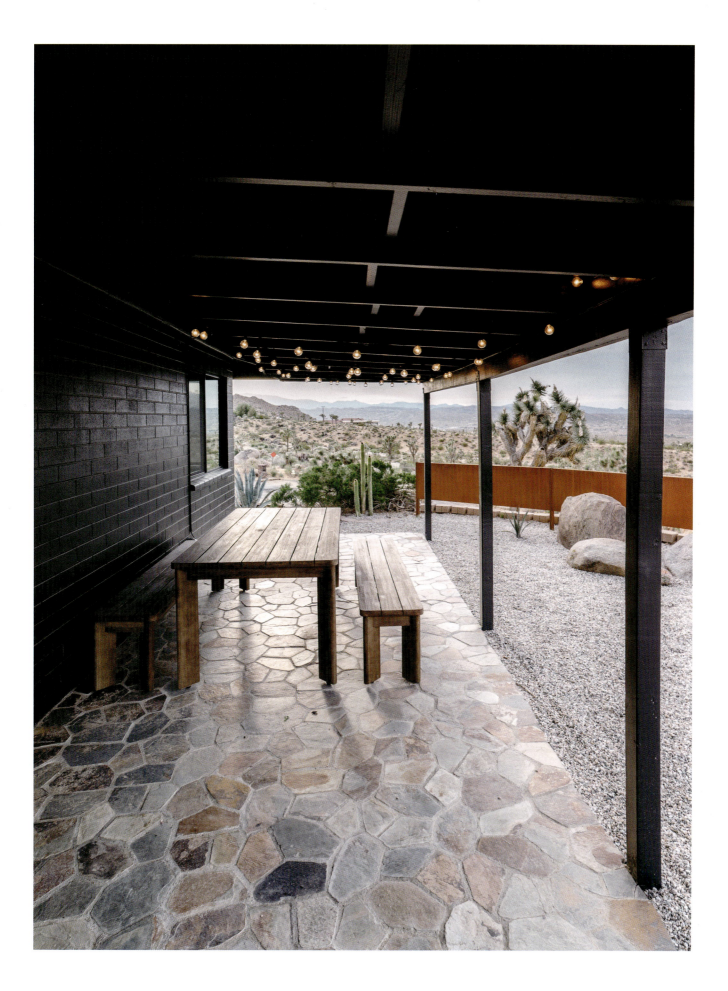

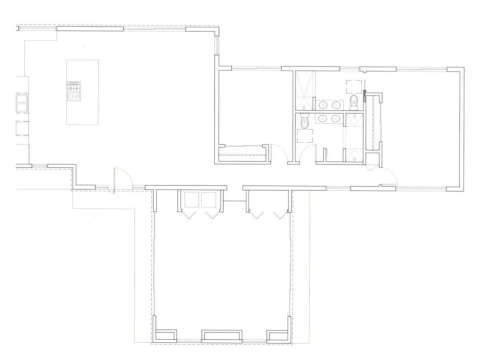

Floor plan

HOUSE RENOVATION IN MONTCADA

Location:
Catalonia, Spain
Area:
1,076 square feet (100 square meters)
Completion:
2019
Design:
Hiha Studio
Photography:
Pol Viladoms

The house is located in an old working-class neighborhood in a city close to Barcelona. All the houses here are from the first quarter of the twentieth century and respond to the standard typology of a ground-floor house—that is, a rectangular plot that is 13 to 16 feet (4 to 5 meters) wide and 33 to 49 feet (10 to 15 meters) long, with a patio at the back. The façades of these houses are very simple and built with basic materials; usually, they only have two openings—the main entrance and either a window or the parking door. The original building of this project was also a house—built in 1925 and then refurbished in the '60s to create a two-bedroom ground-floor house. None of the bedrooms had a window, ventilation, or illumination. Also, there was no patio at the back of the plot.

This update connects the living area to a new patio situated in the back of the plot, which provides a maximum flooding of natural light into the home, while also maintaining the intimacy of the interior space. The strategy that enables this lies in the distinctive corridor which connects the entrance and living area through a curved shape. This curved volume transforms the usually linear and monotonous movement, typical of this typology, into a dynamic one, as it guides the circulation within the space. Inspired by the works of large-scale sculptor Richard Serra, this curved volume endeavors to mimic the impression of moving through the gargantuan folds and turns of his sculptures, and adamantly avoids linear visuals that would usually have been the choice in most other houses. The doorways enlarge the field of view and dissolve all spatial borders to develop a continuous space.

The composition of the façade is based on three rectangular apertures: a ceramic lattice—which makes up two of the apertures—benefits privacy, and the main door makes the third. Covered in the same lattice pattern of the first two apertures, the door supports the impression of the symmetry of the lattice screens.

The materiality of the house is anchored with ceramic elements that stand in contrast with the neutral character of the cabinetry and furniture. Painted white, the walls and ceiling contrast and complement the rich honey tones of the floor tiles, while light-gray furnishing accents beneath the curved excess of the ceiling extend the continuity and the weight of the curved volume.

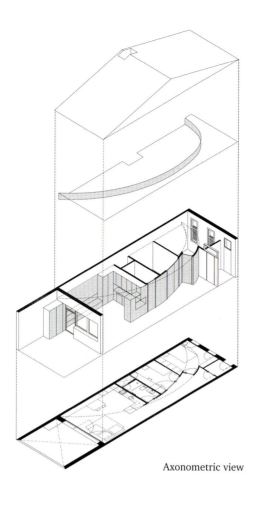

Axonometric view

Floor plan

Section

THE FURNISHED VOID

Location:
Barcelona, Spain
Area:
753 square feet (70 square meters)
Completion:
2016
Design:
Egue y Seta
Photography:
Vicugo Foto

It's not only paint, textures, and furniture that have been selectively curated to embellish the spotless white interior of this flat in Barcelona's Eixample district. The movement of the inhabitants in their daily activities, passing through the space, has also been considered as an active adornment.

The open-plan layout delights in an abundance of natural light that enters through the windows. The home is essentially a "cozy void" that has been functionally resolved to house, and give prominence, to a small but interesting collection of furniture, art, and literature gathered by its young owners.

Their most valuable "acquisition" over the years, though, is not any of the original prints hanging on the walls, nor any of the contemporary classics in industrial design that dot the monochromatic integrated spaces; it is their son, who has managed to colonize every room of the house with a whole lot of "stuff" that is undoubtedly less expensive, but certainly a lot more colorful, resistant, and fun, calling for a rethink of conventional design approaches.

"Toy-proofing" the interior is achieved as a result of questioning the leading role of the built surrounding within the domestic realm, while posing the opportunity to raise questions: Can the "oh-so-sacred" architecture be a mere backdrop to the "true, starring design objects"? How can the background become the figure while remaining at the "back"? The answers are in the clear, practical, and slightly playful and simple solution that is this home: a bright, neat, and comfortable backdrop, that through the random insertion of powerful splashes of color, becomes the object, the frame, or the background, depending on the occasion, the aim, and the focus the viewer chooses to adopt.

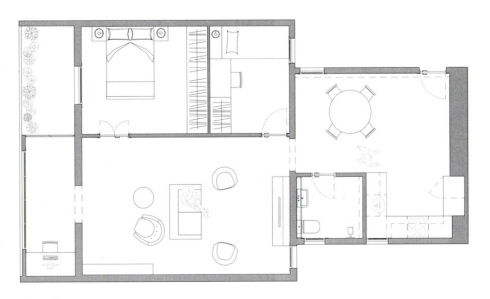

Floor plan

PHOTOGRAPHER'S HOUSE

Location:

London, United Kingdom

Area:

2,530 square feet (235 square meters)

Completion:

2018

Design:

Hugh Strange Architects

Photography:

David Grandorge

This renovation transforms an existing three-story house in Peckham with an extension that creates a bigger home for its inhabitants, while allowing interaction with the outdoors. Following the development of railway connections into central London, the area surrounding this house established itself in the mid-1800s as an attractive suburb, with the local housing stock composed primarily of parallel terraces. Nestled in the middle of one of these Victorian rows, the sizable house contained lower floors that were relatively constrained, as well as largely unconnected with the garden space to the rear.

The upper and lower ground floors are reconfigured completely to design entirely new shared spaces orientated toward the garden; the upper level, where the bedrooms and bathrooms are situated, remains mostly untouched. Extending outwards and downwards creates additional space and height, and the existing cellar is remade and developed to provide connected ancillary accommodation. The structure of the upper ground-floor level has been removed at the rear, allowing a double-height space for the kitchen below, and a connecting stair between the two halves of the house. An inner court channels natural light into the depth of the space that features an easy and relaxed layout.

A new steel frame provides the structure for the expansive new space and also supports the main body of the house above. Contrasting with the gridded uniformity of the frame is custom joinery in Larch tri-board, which provides both built-in and freestanding furniture. While defining the space as part of a whole, almost blending into the outline, these pieces also stand as independent figures that delineate spaces and announce functions. They also add variance to a cool pallor of white and stone-gray. Central to the scheme's architectural focus are the relationships between the house and the garden, and between the steel frame and the joinery.

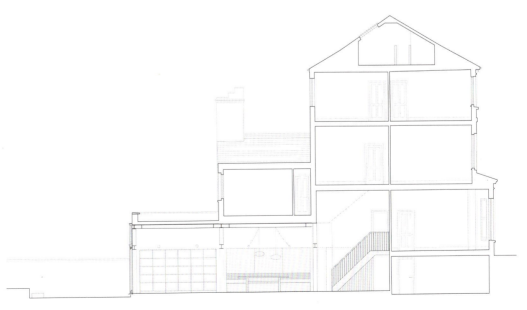

Section

233

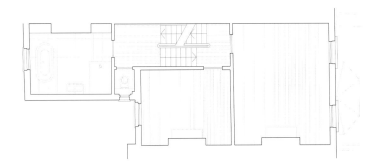

Second-floor plan

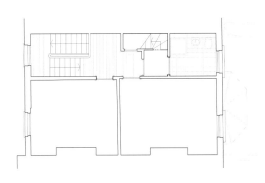

Third-floor plan

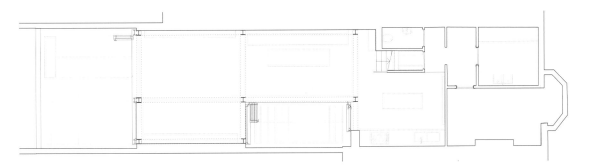

First-floor plan

INDEX

Alts Design Office
P096
www.alts-design.com

Archer + Braun
PP026, 060
www.archerandbraun.com

Atelier Loowe Inc.
P196
www.loowe.jp

Austin Maynard Architects
PP032, 148
www.maynardarchitects.com

Camp Design Inc.
PP132, 172
www.camp-archi.com

COA Associados
P068
www.coa.arq.br

Egue y Seta
P226
www.egueyseta.com

FLOW Architecture
P086
www.flowarchitecture.co.uk

Francesco Pierazzi Architects
P158
www.fparchitects.london

Hiha Studio
PP018, 220
www.hihastudio.com

Hugh Strange Architects
P232
www.hughstrange.com

INchan atelier Co., Ltd.
P188
www.inchan-atelier.com

Jamison Architects
P010
www.jamisonarchitects.com.au

Jost Architects
P052
www.jostarchitects.com

MAGRITS

P086

www.magrits.com

MINI INNO

P206

www.miniin.no

Nic Owen Architects

P114

www.nicowenarchitects.com.au

Nong Studio

P104

www.nong-studio.com

Paulo Martins Arquitectura & Design

P122

www.paulomartins.com.pt

Peter Legge Associates

P042

www.plaarchitects.ie

SHED Architecture & Design

P076

www.shedbuilt.com

Shimpei Oda Architect's Office

P196

www.oda-arc.com

Studio 17 architectes

P166

www.studio-17.ch

Tomomi Kito Architect & Associates

P178

www.tomomikito.com

Zero Studio

P140

www.facebook.com/zerostudioofficial

Published in Australia in 2022 by
The Images Publishing Group Pty Ltd
ABN 89 059 734 431

Offices

Melbourne
Waterman Business Centre
Suite 64, Level 2 UL40
1341 Dandenong Rd, Chadstone,
Victoria 3148
Australia
Tel: +61 3 9561 5544

New York
6 West 18th Street 4B
New York, NY 10011
United States
Tel: +1 212 645 1111

Shanghai
6F, Building C, 838 Guangji Road
Hongkou District, Shanghai 200434
China
Tel: +86 021 31260822

books@imagespublishing.com
www.imagespublishing.com

Copyright © The Images Publishing Group Pty Ltd 2022
The Images Publishing Group Reference Number: 1593

All diagrams and plans are supplied by the participants, and photography is attributed throughout the book, with the following exception: page 4: Stanley Yang Photography (Villa Kuro, MINI INNO).

All rights reserved. Apart from any fair dealing for the purposes of private study, research, criticism or review as permitted under the Copyright Act, no part of this publication may be reproduced, stored in a retrieval system or transmitted in any form by any means, electronic, mechanical, photocopying, recording or otherwise, without the written permission of the publisher.

 A catalogue record for this book is available from the National Library of Australia

Title: Residences Reimagined: Successful Renovation and Expansion of Old Homes
Author: Francesco Pierazzi (Introduction)
ISBN: 9781864709001

Printed by Everbest Printing Investment Limited, in Hong Kong/China

IMAGES has included on its website a page for special notices in relation to this and its other publications. Please visit www.imagespublishing.com

Every effort has been made to trace the original source of copyright material contained in this book. The publishers would be pleased to hear from copyright holders to rectify any errors or omissions.
The information and illustrations in this publication have been prepared and supplied by Francesco Pierazzi and the contributors. While all reasonable efforts have been made to ensure accuracy, the publishers do not, under any circumstances, accept responsibility for errors, omissions and representations, express or implied.